@RAMSeries

@MyLoveThinks

Check out the blog:

www.MyLoveThinks.com

Online Courses:

www.MyLoveThinks.com

555 North El Camino Real Suite A 272
San Clemente, CA 92672
www.RAMSeries.com
www.LoveThinks.com
www.MyLoveThinks.com

All Scripture quotes are used by permission:

Holy Bible, New Living Translation (NLT). 1996, 2004, 2015 by Tyndale House Foundation.

The Holy Bible, New International Version (NIV). 1973, 1978, 1984, 2011 by Biblica, Inc.

Holy Bible: Easy-to-Read Version (ERV). 2001 by World Bible Translation Center, Inc.

The New Testament in Modern English by J.B Phillips (Phillips). 1960, 1972 J. B. Phillips. Administered by The Archbishops' Council of the Church of England.

The Message (MSG). Copyright © 1993, 1994, 1995, 1996, 2000, 2001, 2002. NavPress Publishing Group.

table *of* contents

the *preface*

One of the greatest joys in my job is to work with the oldest of my two daughters, Morgan. Although I would have loved to have both of my girls on board, Jessica, our younger daughter, chose the distinguished profession of medicine and works as a nurse practitioner in a functional medicine practice in New York city.

Morgan jokes that she was learning the craft of psychology at age six when I took her on her "special days with dad," attending classes at the university while I was working on my doctoral degree (with a little creativity, you can make just about anything fun for kids). Little did I know that she would graduate from that same Ph.D. program 20 years later.

Somewhere around her junior year in high school, I asked her to join me when I presented my *How to Avoid Falling in Love with a Jerk (or Jerkette)* program in various conferences, churches, and training sites. She attentively sat through my presentations, ran my booths, and eventually, answered questions about my programs.

What began as a part-time quest to provide a preventative relationship program to singles eventually grew to overshadow my 25-year private counseling practice. By 2010, I had developed and trained over ten thousand instructors who have taught my relationship programs for married couples, parents, families, and individuals to over a million participants. All my programs are built around a theoretical and practical model I developed of the five major bonds that exist in all relationships. You will learn about this Relationship Attachment Model, or the RAM throughout this book.

Morgan continued to work with me throughout her college and graduate studies, with her area of concentration on close relationships. In fact, her doctoral dissertation was a validity study on the RAM. And earlier, she had been the lead author on a research article on the use of the RAM in my singles program, PICK— an article that was awarded the best research article of 2008 by the journal publishers.

During this 20-year adventure, I formed the company, Love Thinks, LLC that is now the brand for all of our relationship materials and services. And to point out the obvious, the name of our organization captures what we believe is essential for all healthy relationships; the heart (love) must work together with the head (thinks).

Morgan has worn many hats with Love Thinks over these years— researcher, developer, graphic designer, public speaker, trainer, and writer. Her Instagram and Blog have become a staple for thousands, with practical and down-to-earth advice for relationships in marriage, dating, and families. It was because of her pithy wisdom that I asked her to put together a section for this book that would give you lots of ideas about how to grow in your relationship through regular couple meetings that we call, your Huddles.

Becoming Better Together is divided into three major sections. In the first section, I explain the guiding principles for building and sustaining healthy relationships. The heart of this book is found in the second section where I wrote two chapters on each of the five major dynamic bonds of your relationship portrayed in the RAM. And the third section, the huddle guide, was written by Morgan to empower you with the skills to intentionally run your relationship, engaging your head with your heart.

Our hope and prayer are that *Becoming Better Together* will provide you with an easy-to-understand plan that is equally easy-to-implement in your relationship. And when you finish reading this book, I would like to challenge you to make a 6-month commitment for weekly huddles. If you do this, your relationship will have to improve, and because you use the RAM in your huddles, you will review and actively strengthen every major area of your marriage relationship. Relationships do not run themselves... they are not self-correcting or self-sustaining. But with this RAM plan, you can be confident that you and your spouse will continue to grow together even though this world is pulling you apart.

the intro-
duction

Introduction: Relationship Goals

Too many of us live by the starvation principle: *feed your relationship only if it is starving*. See if this sounds familiar.

Life has become hectic with your children's schedules, your jobs, projects around the house, and everyday unexpected demands. At some point, you realize that you are completely out of touch with your spouse. This may have surfaced when you saw your spouse playing with the kids, or taking out the trash, or just climbing into bed and you thought to yourself, "Who are you?! It has been so long since we just did something together, just the two of us. We have not even had any time to talk, other than to coordinate schedules."

So, you put out the effort to get a sitter, make the house presentable, prepare a quick dinner for your kids, and shower and dress for your "date night." However, as you pull out of the driveway and finally exhale, the car becomes silent. You have forgotten how to talk with each other. And you feel so distant, that talking to your spouse is actually awkward.

Thankfully, when you arrive at the restaurant, you are rescued by bumping into a couple you know. This couple happens to be the most dysfunctional couple within your circle of friends. By the way, always have one really dysfunctional couple in your network... you know, those people who make you feel really good about your own relationship!

"Did you see how he snapped at her?" You ask.

"I know—you never do that with me... I am so glad you are not like that," your spouse replies.

Your appreciation for your spouse grows as you are waiting for your food, and one thing leads to another, and before you know it, your conversation has reignited.

By the time you have eaten dinner together, taken a walk in the park and watched the sunset, or caught a movie, you walk back to your car, playfully flirting, and feeling like a couple again. But when you pull back in your driveway, you stop the car and look at each other, and say what every couple says after having fed their starving relationship: "We have got to do this more often."

But the next day begins another whirlwind of life that never seems to slow down... and you end up not taking time for each other until you are again starving. Couples that live by the starvation principle have an unspoken belief that if they take care of everything in their life and children's lives, then their relationship will take care of itself. And if it is out of sorts, then in time, it will fix itself. But it never really does fix itself until they reach that point of exasperation and finally, set a goal to do something to feed their relationship.

Relationship Assumptions

> **Healthy relationships are always in a state of balancing.**

Relationship goals. As soon as you put the word, "goals" with the word, "relationships," you immediately create a few assumptions. And interestingly, these assumptions about relationships are the core tenets of this entire book. So, let me briefly point them out, and then in the next few chapters, I will expand on them.

First, when you say that you are making a goal for your relationship, you assume that there is something that needs to be gained, achieved or improved, that something is lacking, and that your relationship needs to be adjusted. And you are right, relationships never reach the finish line; they are never perfect. **Relationships are never balanced.**

Relationships are never balanced.

I like to say that healthy relationships are always in a state of balancing. In fact, it is only as soon as you stop balancing, that you become imbalanced! The idea of being balanced implies that you have arrived at some ideal state, some destination of completeness. But life has a way of interrupting routines with the unexpected. And then, those unexpected things of life impact your relationship, creating new needs and wants, unforeseen obstacles, and demands on your time and energy. So, what do you do? You come together and decide to review all that is happening and set some new goals. Why? Because once again, life has imbalanced your relationship.

Second, when you say that you are making goals for your relationship, you assume that you have some role in running and managing that relationship. You are right! **Relationships do not run themselves!**

Relationships do not run themselves.

You cannot control everything that happens to you or your spouse, but you can be involved in directing your relationship, in charting out where you would like it to go—things you want to do together, ways you want to be closer, skills you want to improve, and dreams you would like to fulfill. The destiny of your relationship is not determined by fate, but rather by the choices you both make about your relationship.

Third, when you say that you are making goals for your relationship, you assume that your relationship needs adjustments. Again, you are right! **Relationships are not self-correcting.**

> # Relationships are not self-correcting.

Basically, this is just the logical conclusion of the first two assumptions. If life keeps unbalancing your relationship, and you are in charge of running your relationship, then you must be the one to take the initiative to improve and strengthen your relationship in the areas where it has been impacted.

So, some of you may be thinking: "God directs my relationship. I am not in control; His will is what I follow." I do not disagree with this, but if you think that submitting to God's will and sovereignty in your life exempts you from any responsibility and involvement in the management of your life, then you have embraced a life-view that contradicts Scripture. Let me give just one example of this from Paul's letter to the Philippian Christians. He instructed them in chapter 2, verses 12-13:

> *Therefore, my dear friends, as you have always obeyed— not only in my presence, but now much more in my absence—continue to work out your salvation with fear and trembling, for it is God who works in you to will and to act in order to fulfill his good purpose.*

Do you see the balance of God's will and Spirit in your life with your responsibility to apply yourself, take charge and "work out" your salvation? If you would replace the word "salvation" with "relationship to God" then it becomes even clearer: "Work out your relationship with God... for it is God who is at work in you."

This blend of God at work in you, as you work out your salvation and relationship to God is found all through the Bible. We are told to be filled or controlled by the Spirit; but then in the very next verse, we are admonished to be sure to "walk" by the Spirit. We are not passive passengers on God's ship of salvation—we are co-workers with Christ, depending on His Spirit and promises as we actively and intentionally run our lives and even our relationship with God.

The vital role you have in running your relationship with God provides a model for your marriage. Your marriage relationship will not run itself. And "depending on God" does not exempt you from actively directing your relationship. You could paraphrase Paul's encouragement to the Philippians as a directive for your marriage: Work out your relationship in marriage with fear and trembling, for it is God who is at work in your relationship to will and to act in order to fulfill his good purpose.

When you put together these three assumptions about your marriage relationship, they lead to only one conclusion: you must have intentional times of meeting together as a couple, so you can assess your relationship, identify what is lacking or desired, and make concrete plans to bring about the needed changes. These meetings are the key to your success in marriage. They are your *relationship management meetings*—and we will refer to them as your huddles.

I could say the same about your relationship with God. You must have regular huddles with God (often referred to as our devotional or quiet times). These are times in which you examine your heart and life to see what is needed or lacking. You then pray, look at the Scriptures and come up with what you should do. And, with the strength and empowerment of God's Spirit, you act on your plan. What is true in your relationship with God is equally true in your relationship in marriage. Relationships do not run themselves, they need to be intentionally directed by you.

Your Relationship Management Meetings: Huddles

If you think about it, all of you have had a "huddle" at one time or another. You may not have called it a huddle or even thought about what you were doing, but I am sure that you have walked through these simple steps... something wasn't going right, and you talked about what was either going wrong or lacking in your relationship. As your conversation (or argument) continued, you identified the things that were lacking or out of balance, and somewhere along the way, you brought up ideas about what would make your relationship better. And as your discussion winded down, you made some promises, a plan of what needs to be done to improve your relationship. If you have ever done anything like this, then you have had a huddle. You have set some relationship goals.

But most couples only have this type of sit-down meeting when one is upset or frustrated in the relationship. So, the idea of a "huddle" comes to be associated with something negative, something to be avoided. However, if you would make these huddles more enjoyable and a regular routine, think how much better your relationship would be. Long before something went seriously wrong, you would have proactively identified what is needed in your relationship, set some goals, and made a plan to actually accomplish those goals.

Relationship Goals

- - - - - - - - - - - - - - - -

Relationship goals. It captures the heart of what is true about relationships—they are constantly fluctuating and needing adjustments to stay strong; they need to be intentionally managed and directed; and unless they are directed and adjusted, they do not self-correct any deficiencies or problems.

This book will provide you with a clear understanding of what exactly is your relationship, how to easily and quickly evaluate the strengths and weak areas of your relationship, and where you should set some goals in order to keep balancing any of the ways that life has imbalanced your relationship. And all of this can be done in a 25-minute, five-step huddle that, over time, will radically improve how you communicate, trust each other, meet each other's most meaningful needs, and enjoy your sexual relationship.

characteristics

of a healthy

relationship

Chapter 1: Your Relationship Is Never Balanced

My wife told me today how much she loved me and missed me. It was when the UPS driver came to the door and I jumped up and said, "Oh, don't let him leave—I need to talk with him." And Shirley, my wife mumbled under her breath, "Isn't he lucky to get a bit of time with you to talk."

Now some of you may think that an off-handed remark like that is a criticism. But I know that it comes from a heart of love that is just struggling with the insanity of a hectic schedule that has squeezed out all of our time to just be together, talking...planning...thinking out loud...and catching up with what has been happening in each of our lives. Let me explain.

We knew that this period of time was going to be stressful because I had just revised seven workbooks used in two of my relationship courses and I needed to update the 350 pages of lesson plans, the power points and redo the twenty-some hours of filming to now match the new changes. All of this needed to be done yesterday in order to have a smooth transition from the previous edition to the new, and we were all geared up to meet the challenge. But then a couple of unforeseen events occurred that took our stress to an entirely new level.

First, our youngest daughter (23 years old at the time) was diagnosed with three pulmonary emboli and hospitalized for two weeks (thank God, she has healed beautifully since then). And then eight days later my step-mom passed away unexpectedly in her sleep. Eight out of the nine siblings and their families converged within a week to mourn this loss. We hosted a number of our out-of-town family members and then provided a memorial dinner for forty in our home. Needless to say, it was a very exhausting and emotional month for all of us with little time for Shirley and me to just be alone together.

But isn't it fortunate that unpredictable times like this are few and far between...NOT! Since this challenging time which occurred several years ago, I frequently think of the tagline: "life comes at you fast" and find myself echoing those words as life speeds up, turns a

> # Just the time you feel like you have a routine working in your relationship...life comes at you fast.

corner, and new challenges emerge. I have become convinced that being balanced is an illusion. Rest assured that in your marriage there is no perfect balance that you attain and then enjoy for the next fifty years. Just about the time you feel that you have a routine that is working in your relationship... life comes at you fast. Couples who have been able to maintain a strong and close relationship over the rocky terrain of life did not accomplish this by achieving some higher order, balanced state that immunized them from the ills of the world.

Too many times, relationships are presented in one of two catgories: healthy or unhealthy, functional or dysfunctional, good or bad! And the implication is that if your relationship is *healthy*, then it will have no deficits or imbalances. This misunderstanding of the **"balanced relationship" is a myth** that conjures up insecurity, guilt and unrealistic expectations in many couples. The truth be known, it is normal for healthy, functional and good relationships to regularly become out of balance.

I can say this confidently; **no marriage is truly balanced.** I would not be surprised if many of you have just breathed your first sigh of relief at the thought that it is normal to be imbalanced. I must admit, I too found relief in accepting that life—and my marriage—is never balanced. A balanced relationship—usually synonymous with the "healthy relationship"—is typically described as a relationship that has no serious deficits.

> **Too many times relationships are presented in one of two categories: healthy or unhealthy.**

In other words, all of the moving parts of the relationship are being attended to in a fairly balanced way. Therefore, what I am calling an "imbalanced relationship" is a relationship that has one or more *deficits* in key areas.

It was **normal** that Shirley and I had three unrelated but overwhelmingly emotional and stressful situations happen at the same time (it is so common that there is an old saying that "bad things come in threes"). It would have been impossible to stay "balanced" in key areas of our relationship over the last couple of months, like our time together, our communication, our romance and most every other area. We became imbalanced because of inevitable deficits that developed as a result of life. That is normal. It is not bad.

In other words, it is just a matter of time before you experience some disruptions in your relationship routine... a birth of a child, a job change, a new stage of parenting, a disability or illness, the loss of a loved one, holiday crazies...the examples are endless. Add to this, you do not remain the same over the years of life. You develop

If there is any guarantee in life, it is that things will change.

different interests, needs, dreams, goals, and perspectives that can drastically impact what you want from your relationship with your partner.

If there is any guarantee in life, it is that things will change... your health, your circumstances, your needs and wants, your goals and ambitions, your children and all of their life situations, your finances, your residences, your vehicles, your styles and your tastes—everything eventually changes, and all of these changes impact your relationship.

It is intriguing to me that this is such a dominant theme in our personal journey with Christ but so overlooked in our relational journey in marriage. In the epistle of James, we read, *Consider it pure joy, my brothers and sisters, whenever you face trials of many kinds, because you know that the testing of your faith produces perseverance. Let perseverance finish its work so that you may be mature and complete, not lacking anything.*

And Jesus warned us in John 16:33 that, *In this world you will have trouble. But take heart! I have overcome the world.* So, we expect trials and troubles in our own personal walk with the Lord. However, when these difficulties occur in our marriage relationships, we tend to look for what is wrong. I think most of you have the expectation that if you just do everything right, then your marriage will be exempt from any difficulties. But you can say with just as much confidence as the prediction that James and Jesus made about your life as an individual, that your marriage is destined to experience many types of trials and troubles in this life.

Unfortunately, most couples actually have the goal to NOT let all of these life events change their relationship. However, I think that this is the wrong approach. First of all, as I have been saying, it is *impossible* to not let all of these changes alter your relationship. Each of you will be impacted by life changes—not just you, but also your partner is impacted by some of the same life events, and most likely by other additional circumstances. So, it is inevitable that changes in life will change your relationship.

However, it is common to interpret changes that spin your marriage relationship out of its orbit as a sign that something is wrong. Maybe you have had these thoughts; "We had a good thing going, but somehow it has been lost... we have drifted... we are no longer close like we used to be and now we seem to be moving in different directions." Although your assessment may be true, your underlying assumption that if your relationship was really healthy, then it would not be impacted by the changes of life is false. Therefore, the crucial question is not if your relationship will change but how will your relationship change, and ultimately, what you will do about these changes.

Chapter 2: Your Relationship Will Not Run Itself

Most couples would give a head nod to the statement, "Marriage relationships take work." But in their day-to-day lives, they do not seem to operate this way. In fact, I suspect that the majority of couples have a deep-seated belief that if a relationship requires "work," then there must be something lacking. They would wonder, "Is our love truly genuine if we must work at it?" There is this romanticized assumption that if you have true love, and your relationship is healthy, then you will not have to "work" at keeping your feelings strong. "Love cannot be manufactured... it either is, or it is not."

> **There is a romanticized assumption that if you have true love and your relationship is healthy, then you will not have to work at keeping your feelings strong.**

I conducted marriage counseling for over twenty-five years. What amazed me was the large number of couples who had no concept of managing their relationship. For most, they had never really thought much about it. Now, don't get me wrong, I am sure that you manage many aspects to your marriage... your finances, your schedules, your work, your recreation, your shopping, your diet, and your fitness (to just name a few areas). However, the "bonds of our relationship," you say. "What is that?"

Running your actual marriage *relationship* is such an abstract concept. What exactly are we running or managing? When it comes to your finances, then you think of your budget. Or, when it is running your schedules, then you imagine checking your calendars to make sure your activities are coordinated. But a relationship, that is something intangible, undefined, and confusing.

Before you had kids, maybe your best talk times occurred while you were cooking dinner together, and then having a relaxing late evening meal. And after your first child, things began to change. You tried to hang onto your special times together, but soon the schedule of your infant began interrupting your couple time.

> **For a couple to maintain a good relationship, they would have to take the time to identify what was lost in their closeness...**

So, I would first point out that this is normal and to be expected. We said in the previous chapter that as life brings changes, your relationship will also be impacted. However, most couples would not take the time to identify what aspects of their relationship were benefitting from their routine, or what personal and relational needs were being met during those meal times. And because they were not tracking their relationship bonds, they would not find some alternative ways to accomplish those same needs. For many couples, this loss of meaningful time together could continue for months and years, eroding their closeness and setting them up for risks in their relationship.

Therefore, for a couple to maintain a good relationship, they would have to take the time to identify what was lost in their closeness, and the ways that they were meeting each other's needs before the birth of their child, and find new ways to accomplish the same end results but with a different relationship plan. However, the erosion of their closeness is so slow that it often occurs undetected.

To be fair, there are those individuals who seem to be natural relationship managers and they practice the art of regularly balancing their relationship without a formal plan or even any awareness of what they are doing. However, these individuals represent a very small minority of people who are married. Plus, they are often frustrated because they are married to a partner who does little to manage the marriage relationship. So, the natural managers begin to feel like they are doing all the planning, initiating, and work in the

> # So, the natural managers begin to feel like they are doing all the planning, initiating and work in the relationship.

relationship.

So, what does it mean to "run your relationship." It may be easier to think of running a relationship in a different setting than your marriage. Imagine being an office manager and one of your primary responsibilities is to keep a positive relationship between you and your staff. What would you have to do to accomplish this? Some of what you would do to manage those relationships is that you would make sure that you know each of your staff fairly well. You would also build a good attitude of trust and respect, clarify roles and responsibilities, make sure they have what they need, and instill a commitment to their work and each other. And, of course, you would be sure to have some form of regular meetings where you can assess what is going well and what is not, evaluate the strengths and weaknesses of your relationships and tasks, and make plans for needed changes and goals to accomplish before your next meeting.

Or, think if you were a coach who is responsible to keep your sports team working together, using the best plays in their offensive and defensive teams, and devising strategies for keeping your athletes fit and performing at their best. You would need to personally know each player, their strengths and weaknesses, their likes and dislikes, and exactly how to bring the best out of them. Like an office manager, you too would want to instill good attitudes of trust and respect, commitment, and the skills of working together. You would want to help them know ways of talking through differences and conflicts, discussing what they need from each other, and strengthening their team bonds. But you would also need a system for evaluating the players on your team; you would need regular meetings with them to discuss where they are in their development and what they specifically need to do to improve; and you would need to have clear criteria to measure their performance and progress. In both the business and sports examples, there is the need to make constant adjustments in response to the identified deficits. There is no room for office ruts or a predictable playbook.

However, most couples are not intentionally evaluating their relationship in this way. And if they did, they would lack a common language to be able to explain what slipped away and how they can bring it back. And anyway, most couples seem to believe that their relationship just runs itself, and when it gets out of balance, it will correct itself.

Chapter 3: Your Relationship Is Not Self-Correcting

The majority of couples that ended up in my office for therapy had a similar story—they had not fixed a longstanding minor leak in the closeness of their relationship. Sometimes this leak had slowly diminished their relationship until it was lifeless and flat. In a few other cases, the slow leak had resulted in weakening significant areas in their relationship that set them up for a major blowout. Remember, slow leaks either lead to flat relationships or big blowouts.

George and Marta were contemplating making an appointment with a divorce attorney when they decided to make that last-ditch effort and see a marriage counselor. Neither seemed very motivated to work at significant changes; both believed that there was not really much hope for retrieving a level of happiness that had alluded them for such a long time. In fact, any marital bliss was so far back in their history that they seriously wondered if it had ever existed.

"When was the last period of time that you can remember being happy and in love with each other?" I asked as Marta squinted her eyes, furrowed her brow and peered into the hazy past to reconnect with what seemed to have become a previous life. George sat motionless as if to yield to Marta's testimony.

"I think that the first couple of years in our marriage we were doing more together—I think we were happier...don't you think so, George?"

"Yea" George agreed and then continued, "I guess that before the kids came we had more time together and did more fun stuff."

"Oooh—that sounds so wrong!" Marta exclaimed. "I don't think that the kids are our problem. It's just that when Sarah was born we spent most of our free time taking care of her. We had been doing lots of things with friends and our summers were spent going out on our boat, but after Sarah, came Jeff; and after Jeff, came Mandy; and somewhere around there we sold the boat because we had not taken it out in years. I think we just drifted apart."

As I continued to conduct an initial interview with George and Marta there surfaced a lack of sex, a lack of communication, a lack of romance and affection, a lack of appreciation, a lack of agreement on how to handle the kids, and an overall lack of emotional closeness. These "lacks" are exactly what I meant by small leaks that eventually flatten a relationship.

George and Marta complained that they had all of these problems in their relationship (sex, communication, no romance, no affection, little agreement) but yet the real problem extended all the way back to the birth of their first child when the routine that was working then stopped working. As I pointed out earlier, it is normal to become imbalanced, and every imbalance creates a small leak in your relationship. The problem is not that you become imbalanced—the problem is when you **stay** imbalanced!

This is worth repeating, it is inevitable that you are going to experience some disruptions in your relationship routine... a birth of a child, a job change, a new stage of parenting, a disability or illness, the loss of a loved one, holiday crazies...the examples are endless. Add to this, you do not remain the same over the years of life. You develop different interests, needs, dreams, goals, and perspectives that can drastically impact what you want from your relationship with your partner. When you do not make ongoing adjustments to the ways that you work together, play together and love together then your small leaks continue and either deflate your relationship (like George and Marta) or threaten to crash your relationship with a big blowout.

Just as a slow leak can flatten your relationship, it can also lead to a big blowout. A prime example is an affair. Now please, do not misunderstand what I am saying. Each of you is always responsible for your own choices and actions, so that it is inaccurate to ever say that your spouse caused you to say or do anything that is wrong, especially an affair.

But with that being said, it is possible to make your partner vulnerable. So, you may not be responsible for causing your spouse to commit an act of infidelity, but you could be responsible for increasing your partner's vulnerability for the attention of another. I have counseled many clients who struggled for years with a partner who refused to talk about much of anything, let alone something personal. As a result, their spouse eventually ceased from asking, and settled for more of a work relationship than a close friendship in

> # The spouse with normal but unmet needs will experience an increased vulnerability to be tempted by someone who would give him/her that attention and interaction.

their marriage. However, the need for closeness and open communication did not cease. And in time, this spouse longed for someone to be interested in the details of their life, to genuinely inquire about the day, and to also share his/her own thoughts and experiences. This unmet need is what I would call a slow leak. As a result, the spouse with normal but unmet needs will experience an increased vulnerability to be tempted by someone who would give him/her that attention and interaction.

There is an interesting Scripture in the New Testament about a couple's sexual relationship and this principle of slow leaks:

> *The husband should fulfill his wife's sexual needs, and the wife should fulfill her husband's needs. The wife gives authority over her body to her husband, and the husband gives authority over his body to his wife. Do not deprive each other of sexual relations, unless you both agree to refrain from sexual intimacy for a limited time so you can give yourselves more completely to prayer. Afterward, you should come together again so that Satan won't be able to tempt you because of your lack of self-control* (1 Corinthians 7:3-5 NLT).

> **When you allow a slow leak to continue in your relationship then you are setting yourself up for big blowouts...**

Do you see the principle of increased vulnerability? No one is responsible for your behavior but you. You cannot blame your partner for your choice to step out of the marriage and engage sexually with another, even when your partner has regularly refused sexual relations with you. However, your partner must accept responsibility for increasing your risk of temptation because of your difficulty with self-control that has resulted from a lack of sexual intimacy within your marriage.

However, infidelity is only one of many major crises that result from a slow leak. Vulnerabilities can develop because you don't have much depth to your con-versations, and your spouse is longing for a meaningful conversation. Or, you want more time together but that never seems to happen. Or you are waiting for your spouse to initiate more re-lational activities like go-ing out, riding bikes, taking walks, having conversa-tions, expressing love and

> **...you need to have a clear definition of exactly what is a relationship.**

appreciation with words, or being more interested in sex. Whenever needs, wants, or wishes continue to be unmet in your relationship, there grows a vulnerability toward someone outside of your mar-riage who would initiate these activities and meet your needs.

When you allow a slow leak to continue in your relationship then you are setting yourselves up for big blowouts like infidelity, finan-cial challenges, secrets, abuses and addictions, online activities, broken promises, neglect, repeated offenses and many other trou-bles of life. Frequently, these big blowouts have percolated over a long period of time in which unresolved minor offenses accumulat-ed, leading to bigger and more serious breaches of trust and respect. This pattern of slow leaks leading to major blowouts accounts for many of the reasons couples initiate counseling, and others initiate divorce proceedings.

So, since it is on your shoulders to run your relationship, to iden-tify the small leaks of closeness in order to strengthen the bonds in your relationship, you need to have a clear definition of **exactly what is a relationship**. In the next chapter, I will provide you with an easy-to-understand, interactive model of your relationship that will help you to know and visualize the major bonds that create closeness. Then you will be able to use that model to accurately identify deficits and imbalances in your relationship, as well as meaningful goals to strengthen your relationship. This model will become your relationship GPS that maps out where you are, and what you need to do to get to where you want to be.

Chapter 4: The RAM

God's plan is for you to grow within the framework of relation-ships and loving others. It is within this framework of relationships with God and others that you grow and mature in your faith, give and receive love, set boundaries, make sacrifices for the good of others, and develop character.

Jesus was cornered by a religious leader attempting to confound him with a trick question in Matthew 22:34-40 (NIV):

Hearing that Jesus had silenced the Sadducees, the Pharisees got together. One of them, an expert in the law, tested him with this question: *"Teacher, which is the greatest commandment in the Law?"*

Jesus replied: *"Love the Lord your God with all your heart and with all your soul and with all your mind.This is the first and great-est commandment. And the second is like it: Love your neighbor as yourself. All the Law and the Prophets hang on these two command-ments."*

It is as if Jesus said, *You can simplify all that God requires of you into two comprehensive commandments...both about love and re-lationships. First, love God. Second, love others.*

Relationships in general, and marriage specifically, have the same primary purpose which is not self-fulfillment, but rather to honor God and fulfill His will in your life! It is a contradiction to believe that you can grow as a Christian while not addressing your relationships. When you grow in your relationship with God, He will help you grow in your relationships with others. And your relationship in marriage and with your children and families are some of the most important and life-changing relationships you will have in this life.

However, have you ever tried to define the word, *relationship?* Usually when I ask this question in a class or seminar, I receive answers that fall in one of two categories. The first is relationship activities like *communication, interaction, commitment.* And the second is relationship types like *marriage, friendship, acquaintances, associates*, or something like, *two people in a union.*

However, the dictionary defines the word relationship simply as a *connection.* A relationship is that invisible connection that occurs between two or more people. However, that does not really tell you a lot. Are there any more specifics or details about what is involved in this connection we call *relationship?*

I have devoted almost all of my career to the development and application of a model of the **specific connections** that make up relationships. Let me trace a bit of my history in trying to create this working model of a relationship. During my graduate studies back in the mid-1980's, I found that there were large bodies of research and theory on major connections or bonds that occurred in relationships. For instance, *trust* was evaluated and used in the titles of over 5,000 published research studies in scientific journals in the last century. It has been included in every major psychological, sociological, and relationship theory, and has been a topic in countless books and articles. Trust is one major way people connect, and in close relationships, it is absolutely vital for developing and maintaining feelings of security, intimacy and safety. But trust was not the only connection I found. In fact, I found four other major connections that have generated similar amounts of research, theory, and practical self-help books!

All five of the major connections I identified had several common features. The first was that they were unique contributors to the feeling of a bond or closeness with another person. In some cases, each major connection was presented as synonymous with intimacy, or emotional closeness, or even love. But in all cases, each of these major connections were clearly shown to be a bond between two or more people.

The second common feature was that they all existed in ranges. Trust, for instance, is not an either/or experience in relationships, but rather it exists in differing levels, from very low to very high trust.

The third feature I found that they all shared was that they were dynamic, fluctuating in their ranges because of circumstances and interactions. They never remained at the same level for long lengths of time. In fact, they seemed to have a natural loss of intensity, like a slow leak, when they were not regularly maintained or intentionally strengthened. For example, trust naturally erodes over time if there is nothing reinforcing it in a relationship.

Finally, these connections all interacted with each other. If one went up in its range of intensity, then it tended to have an upward pull on the others. In contrast, if the intensity of one dropped, then it seemed to pull the others in that same direction. And when one or more were significantly higher than some of the others, then conflicting feelings of closeness and distance occurred in the relationship.

Therefore, I knew I needed to develop a model that visualized these five major connections, while also capturing the ways they interact and fluctuate. I wanted this model to be true to this large body of theory and research, but also easy-to-understand and interactive. I designed the major connections or bonds of relationships as five channels on a mixing board, with each one having a similar range. The level of development or intensity of each relationship bond would be represented by how far the slider was moved up.

I called my model the Relationship Attachment Model, or RAM for short (see figure 4.1). Together, these five connections provided a visual, interactive portrayal of the five invisible bonds that comprise all of your relationships. And because it is interactive, you can easily **profile** your relationship to depict the specific strengths as well as the areas of deficit.

Figure 4.1

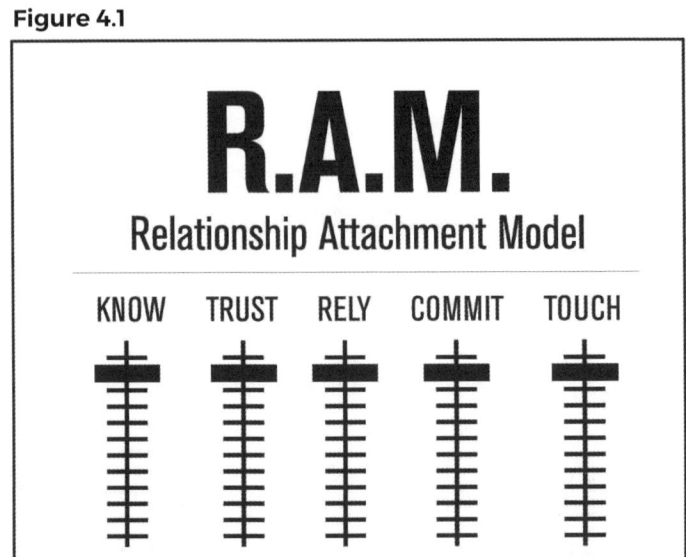

Over the past three decades, the RAM has been empirically validated in both qualitative and quantitative research studies. It has been taught and used in social agencies, faith communities, educational settings like high schools, undergraduate and graduate programs, counseling practices, and imbedded in the curricula I have developed that have been taught to over a million participants.

If the truth be known, relationships are complicated. It is no wonder that most couples do not give a lot of thought about managing their relationship bonds... *What does that even mean?* most would ask. That is why a model that portrays the invisible and dynamic bonds of your relationship will be so helpful and empowering to you. You can also think of these dynamic bonds as five strands that are braided together to form the overall relationship cord that connects you with another. Although each one is separate and distinct, they are intertwined into a global connection we call "relationship."

Let me briefly introduce each of these five dynamic bonds. As I previously mentioned, these relationship bonds can fluctuate in a range from high to low. So, as I describe each one, I will make some references to how they are impacted by different situations and relationship experiences.

##

The first bonding connection is the degree that you **know** your partner. Your first reaction may be, *What are you talking about—I know my partner.* But I am referring to the ways you share your thoughts, dreams, feelings and experiences from day to day—so that you can truthfully say, *my partner knows me better than anyone else.* This kind of knowing requires quality communication, but it also necessitates enough *quantity* of time together to move from surface chit chat to more meaningful sharing.

Obviously, this level dropped significantly in my marriage during those two months I described in a previous chapter when Shirley and I had to deal with my increased work load, my step-mother's death, and our youngest daughter's life-threatening attack of three pulmonary emboli. It was normal for us to become absorbed with others during that time and to have little time just for each other. This created mixed feelings—on the one hand, greater closeness was generated from going through shared emotional experiences. But on the other hand, there were feelings of distance from our lack of attention to each other.

It is normal when we go through times like that, for our relationships to feel out of sync. And so, when the realities of life alter your communication and time together, then you will feel a bit disconnected with each other, as if you don't really know what your partner has been thinking and feeling, and maybe even out of touch with what your partner has been facing day to day. On the RAM, the know slider would be lowered to represent this distancing in your relationship.

Everyday experiences can also impact how you are staying in the know, as well as all of the five bonds in your relationship. For instance, your job requires extra hours because of some project that has a deadline that is looming over you. Next thing you know, you are consumed by the stress and tasks involved in the mad race to finish this project on time. You have little energy for your children, and even less for your spouse. When you cross that finish line and take a moment to look around, you realize that there is a great distance that separates you from your spouse. You are not sure what your spouse has been going through for the last few weeks. You are *out of the know*—and even though your spouse may completely understand, and even though this rat race was inescapable, your *know* level has still dropped. This may be normal, but the key to keeping your relationship healthy is that you recognize this distance and together, strengthen the bonds that were impacted by life. This is how the RAM can help! It provides a mirror for you to see where you are in your relationship, and a common language to talk about how to move forward.

Trust

The second dynamic bond described in the RAM is the **trust** you have for your spouse. Most of you will immediately think that trust only refers to keeping your vows and staying faithful. Although this is absolutely essential, trust actually involves so much more. Trust is your feeling of confidence and security that flows from what you *think* of your partner. As you have grown to know your partner, you have taken what you know and put it together in an opinion, a mental portrait of your spouse. Technically, your feelings of trust do not come from what you know, but from what you *think about* what you know.

Maintaining a secure trust in each other is crucial to the strength of your relationship. This means that you must keep a positive attitude toward your spouse, focusing on their strengths, minimizing their weaknesses, forgiving their faults, and rebuilding your belief in them when it has been damaged.

But trust also requires trustworthiness. Trust expects your spouse to be there for you, to step up when needed, and to do what they said they were going to do. Your trust is your feeling of assurance that flows from what you think and believe about your spouse.

This leads us to reliance, the third dynamic bond in your relationship and represented in the RAM. **Rely** refers to the ways that you depend on each other to meet each other's needs and wants, to work together to fulfill life responsibilities, and to love and play together, creating enjoyable and memorable experiences. Trust is more about what you think of your spouse, whereas reliance is more about what you do for your spouse.

When my daughters were growing up, they took their grades seriously. One of the things they both despised in school were those group projects in which their grade would be determined by the entire group. One afternoon, my youngest, Jessica walking through the door after school with a scowl on her face.

> "What's wrong?" I asked.
> "I was assigned to work in a group with Sammie. And she never does her part. And our grade will be a group grade. So I am going to get a B or C, all because of Sammie. It is NOT fair!"

Jessica knew Sammie well enough to know that she could not be trusted to pull her weight; her **know**-level of Sammie was high, her **trust**-level was low, but here is the rub, Jessica's **rely**-level was really high... she had to rely on a group member that she did not trust. And that drove her crazy.

You see, Jessica's trust was more about what she thought of Sammie, whereas her reliance was more about how she had to interact and depend on Sammie. In your marriage relationship, maintaining a trust and belief in each other is vital, but it needs to be reinforced with the actions of reliance.

For years, when I taught the session on reliance in my Couple LINKS course, I would divide the couples into two groups (men and women) and have them generate a top-ten list of what husbands and wives want from their spouses. The twist came when I asked the women to brainstorm what husbands want from their spouses, and asked the men to figure out what wives want from their partners. The idea behind this was to make men and women think from a perspective different than their own. I wanted the women to think like men, and the men to think like women.

For spouses to accurately meet each other's needs, it is vital that each spouse is clear about what their partner wants and needs. This requires getting into the world of your partner, and learning to love them in ways that are most meaningful to them, and not necessarily you. The level of reliance in your relationship is determined by the extent that you are able to depend on your partner to do this.

Commit

The fourth dynamic bond in your relationship is the extent that you **commit** yourself to your partner. Some of you may think that commitment was only the promises you made at the altar those many years ago. But think of commitment as having three dimensions: promise, priority and presence. First, commitment is a decision, a vow, a promise. There may be times when you do not feel like following your commitment, but yet you stick with it because of your promise. A traditional wedding is really all about the sharing of vows. For millennia, marriage has been understood as the ultimate commitment, *until death do us part.*

But commitment is also a priority. There are some who have stayed true to their promise, and yet do not put their marriage or the needs of their spouse as a priority in their life. So, on the RAM, you could portray their commitment by moving the slider to the top when it comes to fulfilling a promise, but drop it to the bottom when it comes to having the priority of fulfilling a spouse.

And third, commitment can be understood as presence, or as

carrying your partner in your heart. Wherever you are, regardless of the separation of time and space, there also, is your partner. Commitment says, *I belong to you and you belong to me. Where you go, I will be there.* Commitment, then is practicing the presence of your partner.

Regularly exercising your commitment in these three dimensions, strengthens the spirit of your resilience which will hold you together when life depletes any or all of the other four dynamic bonds described in the RAM. Keeping your promise to be completely committed in your heart, practicing the presence of your partner, and keeping your spouse a priority while putting their interests above your own will definitely pull your relationship through life's valleys.

Touch

The fifth dynamic bond in your relationship is **touch**. Your romance, affection, chemistry and entire sexual relationship is a major source of closeness and intimacy. Even the chemicals that are produced in your brain during sexual arousal (e.g. oxytocin, dopamine and vasopressin, to name a few) are known for their bonding effects. However, like the other four connections that make up your relationship, your affection and sexual activity will fluctuate with alternating times of passion and disinterest, closeness and distance, frustration and rekindling.

So, the RAM provides an interactive representation of what is happening in your relationship in the five major sources of your feelings of closeness and bond. It will help you to navigate your marriage when you encounter the unexpected, to identify which area of your relationship has been impacted, and to profile these changes in a visual way. It provides you with a common language so that you can talk through where you are, where you want to go, and how to get there.

The RAM provides you with a job description that you can use to intentionally run your relationship and set realistic relationship goals. It can be used to define what areas of your closeness need to be strengthened. The RAM is like your relationship GPS: it reflects the present location of your relationship, the distance between where you are and where you would like to be, and it can be used to generate a plan for setting mutual goals to navigate your relationship toward your chosen destination.

Chapter 5: Huddles

When I was growing up, the annual family-and-friends football game was the highlight of our Thanksgiving celebration. The day seemed to drag on forever as my mother coordinated the kitchen crew who rushed around feverishly to bring to a perfectly-timed crescendo the feast of a thousand dishes. You learned to go out of your way to avoid the kitchen lest one of the many mother figures (Grandmas, older sisters, Aunts and any other females who felt a sense of maternal entitlement) would catch your eye and recruit you for an endless string of domestic tasks.

Meanwhile, my brother-in-law led the fanatical fans of husbands and boys at the *Tele-Bowl* in hours of screaming, groaning, jumping and cheering for the favored team as if the television had transported them directly inside the stadium. Me? I had been dressed since breakfast in my football attire: pads, spikes and helmet—repeatedly throwing the football up and catching it in a game-winning dive onto the living room carpet as I waited for the announcement that everyone was to take the field for the annual Thanksgiving game.

Now if you were smart, you would make sure you were picked by the team that my father was on. He was the perennial quarterback that always had that crucial, fourth-down play that instructed every player to do something to distract the defense while the least likely player would march the ball across the goal.

What I find funny now that almost fifty years have passed since that wonderful era of life, is that I don't even remember specifics about those games... like who won, or what the score was, or who was on my team. But the one image that is crystallized in my memory is the huddles with my Father. He always seemed to be able to scrutinize the defense in order to figure out their weaknesses and within a split second, devise the most elaborate play. I remember running back to the huddle all excited for what was going to come next. It seemed that each move of the defense had an equal but opposite countermove in his unwritten offensive playbook. In every huddle, he made adjustments in response to whatever was needed or lacking in the last play series just like the contemporary quarterbacks who step up to receive the snap, but then change the play based on the configuration of the defense.

As obvious as it is for managers and quarterbacks to have regular huddles for setting the next strategy or play, you would think that couples would have taken up this practice as a norm for running a marriage. And yet, only a few couples take the time to regularly review their relationship and set small goals that will adjust the most important areas of their intimacy in ways that better meet each other's needs.

> **Couples who have some sort of a huddle usually stumbled upon it rather than making it an intentional decision.**

Couples that have had some sort of a huddle have usually stumbled upon it rather than making an intentional decision. Let me describe a typical day in the life of a married couple. You are driving together to attend your nephew's wedding when, off the cuff you ask, "So, where are they honeymooning?"

Your spouse describes their upcoming exotic, two-week hon-eymoon to Barbados after which you murmur under your breath, "Must be nice."

This sets off a discussion about the extensive amount of time since your last real vacation. Yes, you took a week off last year and visited your parents... and the year before you had a renovation-va-cation when you refurbished your 80's décor; and all the previous years seemed to be child-centered trips—Disney, camping, grand-parents, Cedar Point and countless other theme parks. But there was a deafening silence when the question was posed: When did we get away—**just the two of us**? And as you moved closer toward your nephew's wedding destination, you moved farther apart in the car.

However, the tension lessened when one of the two of you broke the silence, "So what can we do about it?" It was then that you both began to brainstorm, to negotiate and ultimately to plan a watered-down version of your nephew and his new bride's bliss-ful honeymoon. By the time you walked in to the chapel you were feeling better about your own relationship and more hopeful about your immediate future.

Most couples have had an experience like this but unfortunately were not cognizant of what they were *actually* doing. If someone asked, the explanation would be given that we were just having an argument; or "a discussion"; or, for the more analytic, that the wed-ding conjured up thoughts and emotions of what marriage ought to be which led us to face what we were lacking. But all of these explanations would have only addressed the moment and not the big picture of your relationship. What you were in fact doing was simply having a huddle! You were reviewing your relationship to identify what was lacking in order to balance your imbalances.

So, if there is one major take-away from this entire book it would be this:

**become committed to meeting together in regular
huddles and using the RAM to help you identify where**

you are in your relationship bonds, what is going well and what is lacking, and then to plan together what is needed to strengthen those areas and rebalance your relationship.

Your marriage is a journey, and the RAM can be your relationship GPS. It can help to locate exactly where you are and the route that can get you to an even better place. Remember that it is normal to become out of balance; that life will impact you, your spouse and your relationship in ways that drain one or more bonds of your closeness. But with the RAM you will have a common language to talk about your relationship without attacking and or becoming overly defensive. And it is in these regular huddles that you will *re-route* your relationship in small ways to ultimately keep you on the course of a healthy and balanced relationship.

Huddles should be brief—only 20-30 minutes. They should remain positive—they are not an opportunity for you to unload on your spouse. Ignore this rule and watch how quickly you stop having huddles.

It only takes a few negative experiences to create a relationship rut. Turn your huddle into a boxing match or a dumping ground of complaints, and you will quickly find that your spouse will do just about anything to avoid getting cornered in another huddle. This is why huddles need to be positive. You should expect that some things will be lacking in your relationship. And the huddle is not about assigning blame, but rather it is about coming together to identify what has been missing, or what new things are desired, and making a short-ranged plan to bring it about.

> **Huddles are not an opportunity to unload on your spouse.**

Your huddle should not be an attempt to fix all the issues you identify. The huddle is more like a planning meeting between you and your spouse. Once you review the last week or two, and share what you appreciate about each other, you identify what you think is lacking or needed to strengthen your relationship as you move forward in the upcoming weeks. If you believe that there is a topic that has not been talked about enough, say, for example, where you will be spending the holidays, then you set a time to talk about this rather than trying to take the entire huddle to discuss this issue. This way, your huddles will not turn down a rabbit trail and end up lasting an hour or more. Even if that *rabbit-trail* huddle was extremely productive, the length of time it required would backfire, instilling apprehension the next time you considered having a huddle.

So, if you keep your huddles positive and brief, then you are more likely to have them frequently. I suggest that you begin by having weekly huddles. It is easier to establish a habit if you make your huddle the same day and time each week. If you want to stretch your huddles out to monthly, then only do that after five or six months of meeting weekly. And I would recommend that you not spread them any farther apart than a month. Remember, the huddle is designed to make small adjustments to your relationship. This requires that you meet frequently to identify what is out of balance *before* too much time has transpired.

If you follow these simple rules, you will find that your huddles are enjoyable and empowering in your relationship. They will begin to happen naturally whenever something needs to be addressed. However, at first, your huddles may feel stiff and awkward. Don't let this bother you. Whenever you attempt to do something new, there is an increase in self-consciousness and a feeling of unfamiliarity. But as you continue weekly huddles, the format will become more automatic, and your comfortability will increase.

So, to make your huddle easy to follow, I am going to use the RAM as the five steps of your huddle. The first two steps are more of a retrospective look back on what has been happening since your last huddle (or over the last week or two). And the last three steps take on a prospective look at what you would like to do before your next huddle.

Here are the five steps to follow in your huddle. As I said, it is as though you are just walking through the RAM beginning on the left with staying in the know, and ending with keeping an affectionate and loving sexual relationship.

> **KNOW**: *Catch Up* about what has happened with each other since your last huddle—anything you need to talk about that you have overlooked or just lacked the time to discuss. If too much to talk about right in your huddle, set a time to get into it. This is also the time to review how you have been staying in the know... do you wish your partner would do or say anything differently to be more inquiring or more disclosing.

> **TRUST**: *Patch Up* your trust-pictures of each other by taking time in every huddle to review the ways that your spouse has blessed you with things they have said and done since your last huddle. And if there were any misunderstandings, conflicts, or breaches of trust, then give and receive your apologies (or affirm again your apology even if you had previously done so), and establish resolutions for rebuilding your feelings of trust. If there have been few or no offenses since the last huddle, then this step is all about recounting the strengths of your spouse and expressing your love and admiration for who they are and what they have done.

> **RELY:** *Dream Up* the things that you would like to do before your next huddle. This is the step that transitions the focus of your huddle from a look back to a look ahead. And because there will always be something lacking, then these deficits become the opportunities for you to give to your

spouse, or to plan enjoyable things to do before your next huddle. Together, you can be connoisseurs of each other, identifying and meeting important needs and wants. And, of course, be sure to put your plans on your calendars! And do not forget the "mundane"—check in with each other to make sure that you are both happy with the ways you have been working together and sharing the division of responsibilities in your home.

COMMIT: *Back Up* each other by looking ahead on your calendars, and finding ways to support each other in your upcoming responsibilities and activities. Support can come in small and large ways, from a simple text, letting your partner know that you are thinking about them, to rearranging your schedule so that you can attend an event that is important to your spouse. This aspect of your commitment also overlaps with how you rely on your partner to help with specific responsibilities and chores. So, look for ways that you can back up your spouse by supporting them in their respective areas of responsibility.

TOUCH: *Build Up* each other by taking some extra time to talk about your affection, romance and sexual intimacy... what you appreciate, and what you would like to do before your next huddle. The sexual relationship is impacted by the other four dynamic bonds of your relationship, along with the many stresses and activities of life. Express your love in words and in affection as you wrap up your time together.

Here is this entire book in one paragraph. Your relationship consists of five major bonds or connections—how your stay in the know with each other, how you keep a secure and positive trust, how you rely on each other to meet your most significant needs, how you keep a strong commitment, and how you maintain a loving and satisfying sex life. These five bonds in your relationship do not run themselves, but they will be impacted and strained by life. Unless you have intentional times of huddling together to identify how they have changed and what needs to be done to rebuild them, they will not correct themselves. And if they remain weakened, then those slow leaks can lead to big blowouts in your relationship. So, take charge of your relationship... use the RAM as your relationship mirror, your GPS, and your steps for your couple huddles; and you will master the art of maintaining a strong bond of love over a lifetime of change.

intentionally

creating a
healthy

relationship

Chapter 6: Know: Developing Open Communication

Tim Keller made an astute observation about intimacy in marriage:

> *To be loved but not known is comforting but superficial. To be known and not loved is our greatest fear. But to be fully known and truly loved is, well, a lot like being loved by God. It is what we need more than anything.*[1]

As we have explained previously, the RAM portrays the major bonds that comprise your relationship. And each one is so vital to the health of your relationship. However, in many ways, the other four builds upon the ways that you and your partner **know** each other—keeping in touch with what your partner is experiencing, whether you are together or apart. This is the cornerstone to a strong and intimate relationship.

When you think of what it means to know someone, you may just think of knowing things *about* that person. This kind of surface knowledge is part of what knowing someone means.

However, the words that are translated *know* in both the Old and New Testament reveal that there is much more.

There are two aspects to the Biblical definition of knowing someone—factual awareness and emotional encounter. What I mean by factual awareness is this: the extent that you truly know someone is determined by how aware you are of the facts of their life: their experiences, feelings, and thoughts.

But this can be a cold, distant and uncaring awareness. The second aspect, an emotional encounter means that you are touched by what you intellectually understand. Your emotions and will are activated. What you "know" may make you feel happy or sad, relieved or agitated, reassured or anxious. But you have an encounter with whatever you have learned. Another way to say this is that you take to heart what you learn about your partner.

In Psalms 139 verses 1-4 we read:

You have searched me, Lord, and you know me. You know when I sit and when I rise; you perceive my thoughts from afar. You discern my going out and my lying down; you are familiar with all my ways. Before a word is on my tongue you, Lord, know it completely.(NIV)

Does this sound like objective and factual knowledge? No, it clearly is a very personal and relational awareness—God is interested in you and His knowing of you, your motives, your actions, your thoughts and words—are all driven by His love and value of you. When you truly love and value someone, you are compelled to deeply and intimately know that person.

In verse 5, the Psalmist exclaims, *You put Yourself behind and before me, and keep Your hand on me.* (MEV) The image is not one of threat but of security. A small child will often become insecure when in a public place and separated or even distanced from a parent. But when the parent is in front and behind the child, when the parent's hand is reassuringly placed on the shoulders of the child, then there is a confidence that replaces fear. We see these two aspects of *knowing* intertwined when the Scriptures describe the way that God lovingly knows everything about you while also making you feel secure in this intimate bond.

God knows that the longing of every human heart is to be known with loving acceptance and genuine value. This is the ultimate stan-

> # You may need to remind yourself to listen to your partner with a greater sense of value and worth, looking beyond the words that are spoken to see the meanings and feelings of what your spouse is really experiencing.

dard of what it means to "know" each other in your marriage relationship. You should cultivate a desire to be in your partner's world, to value and appreciate all that your spouse experiences; to feel their feelings, to know their thoughts, and to walk in their shoes.

I must admit, I am a little humored by the phrase, *and before a word is on my tongue, you Lord, know it completely.* This kind of sounds like my wife and how she seems to know what I am going to say before I even say it. But, to her credit, she is tracking what I am talking about, while she seems to be experiencing in her mind and heart the yarn I am spinning. If she was a bit dismissive and condescending when I talked with her—like, "Yeah, yeah...I know what you are going to say next, so hurry up, get on with it." Then her knowledge of me would be without any heart, value or love. But instead, I can usually see on her face all my unspoken emotion as I explain something going on in my life.

Let me give you another example of these two aspects of knowing from the life of Jesus. In the Gospel of Matthew, chapter 6 verses

25-32, Jesus reassures his disciples that they do not need to worry about food, clothing, or housing. As a flock of birds flew over their heads, he looked up at them and pointed out that they were not flying around, storing up lots of food for the future. They seemed to know that God would daily provide what they needed. He then, turned their attention to the lilies in a field and amusingly deduced that the flowers do not spend their days making their outfits, yet Solomon in all his glory did not look as stunning as they do. And to bring his point home, Jesus explained that these flowers are enjoyed today and then thrown in the trash tomorrow. In other words, God values you way beyond these other examples of nature. So, if God cares so much for the natural world, how much more will He care for you, His own child.

> ...good habits take much longer, and always seem to require many more times of reinforcement.

Jesus summarized with one simple but profound truth everything He had taught about the security you can feel when you fully understand the value and love God has for you: *Your heavenly Father knows that you have need of all these things* (verse 32). This knowledge is not an uncaring awareness. It is an expression of the extent that God values you. He is both deeply aware and touched by what He knows about you and your needs. God considers you precious, and everything He knows about you is tempered by the priceless worth you hold in His eyes.

This is how you grow in knowing each other through the years of your marriage. You share your experiences, thoughts and feelings with a partner who hears and understands the content of what you are saying, while also valuing and taking to heart what it really means to you. We are all guilty from time to time of slipping into the rut of just catching up with the kids' activities and schedules, bills and other obligations, and reciting the events of the day in a business-like manner with little concern or interest in each other. But when this happens, we are no longer *in the know* and the content of what you share has become impersonal, with little to no focus on what each other is going through, thinking and feeling.

Therefore, it is important to regularly refresh your attitude and shift your perspective when you talk together. You may need to remind yourself to listen to your partner with a greater sense of value and worth, looking beyond the words that are spoken to see the meanings and feelings that your spouse is really experiencing.

A primary way to ensure that you stay in the know is to have regular talk times. Unless you make it a priority to take time to step out of the rush of life and talk together, you run the risk of losing track of consistent face-to-face talks. This does not have to be a *sit-on-the-couch"* and *"stare in each other's eyes* encounter. Many have had their best talk times during dinner preparations, or talking over a meal, or cleaning up after the kids have gone to bed, or walking the dog. The key is to minimize distractions, and have a focused and consistent time of talking about what is really going on in your lives.

I remember watching an episode of Everybody Loves Raymond. Ray and Debra were sitting on the couch as Ray settled in for countless hours of watching sports. Suddenly, the cable went out, and after Ray made every attempt to reconnect to his beloved sports station, he resigned himself to starring at the fuzz on the television screen.

Debra clicked off the TV and questioned, "Ray, Can't we just sit here and talk."

"Why?" Ray retorts, "What's wrong?"

"Nothing is wrong". Debra explains. "When was the last time we just sat here and talked?"

"The last time something was wrong!" Ray complains.

It is all too easy for your talk time to become your gripe time. And as soon as that happens, you will stop having regular talk times. Make sure to stay positive, and if you slip into a time of criticism, negativity or arguing, get back on track and reestablish a warm and enjoyable conversation. Typically, bad habits are formed very quickly, needing only two or three experiences to establish a pattern. But good habits take much longer, and always seem to require many more times of reinforcement.

When you have a talk time, weave together your situational and relational domains of experiences. In other words, the different circumstances and situations you have encountered, and the ways that you and others have interacted in relationships become the content of what you talk about.

As you both continue to *stay in the know*, there will be times that you delve deeper in your communication. Your openness in communication can be measured by four depths in these relational and situational domains. These depths range from shallow to deep, and most topics extend through all four layers.

For instance, it is common for you to revisit the same topics time and time again, but often at different depths. You may talk with your spouse about your experiences within your family of origin with minimal depth at one point, but then in another conversation you talk much more openly. And then, with additional family experiences, you end up sharing even more than before. We never fully know each other in marriage, and as soon as we catch up on our current events, more of life occurs generating more things to share.

It is helpful to categorize the different levels of openness in communication. Over the years of communication theories, there have been many descriptions for these depths of openness. I use a simple acronym, OPEN, to characterize the four major levels.

1. **Observations and facts**—these refer to the type of communication where you relay current events, estab-

lished facts, and things you've heard and seen. "I had a tough day at work today," is an example of communicating on this level.

2. Perspectives and opinions—they describe the type of communication where you add interpretations and opinions to your facts. "I think my supervisor overlooked the work I did for her on the project, which was not fair."

3. Experiences and emotions—these convey more of the subjective, personal, and emotional content about your facts and opinions. "I feel angry that my supervisor did not credit me for any of the work I did for her—it was her project, but I did most of the work. And when she presented it, she acted like it was all her work. But I also feel trapped that if I say anything, then it will come back to bite me."

4. Needs and relationship responses—this deepest level of communication occurs when you put your deepest feelings into words. Both refer to a here-and-now experience where you convey feelings you are having at that time about either something very personal or some way you feel toward the person you are with. "I don't really want any advice from you right now... just for you to listen and understand what I have been going through at work. I think I just need to vent for a bit and then I will feel better... and I feel really supported and cared for by you, because you were such a good listener."

Healthy relationships continue to cycle through the same topic areas from the situational and relational domains, yet with more meaning and depth each time. Being aware of both what you share, and the depth of your openness helps you to keep track of how you are staying in the know.

Periodically, talk about your talk times, and how you are talking together... talk about your talk! Make sure that you both feel that you are talking through topics that are meaningful and important to each of you, and avoiding the rut of just having shallow conversations. Staying in the know is the cornerstone of true intimacy. To feel loved and known is the longing of the human heart, and your communication is a major means to the end of fulfilling this need.

Chapter 7: Know: Maintaining Empathetic Communication

Before you even get through the first chapters of the first book of the Bible, you discover the deeper significance of what God intended for married couples in how they know each other. Genesis 4:1 stated that *Adam knew Eve, and she conceived...* indicating that the sexual act was much more than just a physical act; it was an encounter and expression of deep intimacy. In this choice of wording for such an intimate act, you see the idea of an experiential bond in the Hebrew understanding of the word, "to know." This meaning is carried on in a figurative way throughout the entire Bible in the many references of how God knows you, how He wants you to know Him, and how He wants you to know each other in your marriage relationship.

To *stay in the know* in your marriage, you must communicate in ways that transport you out of your own perspective and into the experiential world of your partner. If you are to make this happen, your listening must be more than the simple act of reciting the words you hear. When you listen with heart, you look for what your partner actually means, and empathize with what your partner is experiencing. Romans 12:15 captures the idea of knowing someone with a genuine and empathetic heart in the phrase, *Rejoice with those who rejoice, and weep with those who weep.*

Healthy communication, then is a means to an end. It must lead to deeply knowing your spouse. This makes communication more than just a behavioral skill that you can be trained to do. It involves your conscience, and your thoughtfulness, compassion, imagination and concentration. Of course, there are techniques for positive communication. But the mastery of communication skills without the cultivation of a heart to genuinely know your partner will ultimately lead to a hollow relationship void of true intimacy.

Staying in the know with each other is incredibly important to maintaining a close, bonded marriage relationship. In a study based on data collected from a 17-year longitudinal study of marital instability, 2,033 married individuals were asked an open-ended question, "What do you think caused your divorce?" Eighteen categories were created from the analysis of responses and four of the eighteen were directly related to the how the couples felt close in knowing each other. For example, the fifth most common reason was that the couple "grew apart" and that their interests and priorities changed, and the seventh most common reason was stated as a communication problem, *We just do not talk anymore.*

These reasons for divorce are directly related to the bonding dynamic of staying in the know. Those who lost their compatibility did not engage in consistent talking and time together to preserve the compatibilities they once had when they entered their marriage, or to develop new ones. Those who *grew apart* did not continue to have close and open communication with their partner.

This idea of *growing apart* as a common reason for divorce is found throughout marriage research. Knowing another and/or being known enhances the relational bond, and contributes to the feeling of closeness in a relationship. However, when this dynamic bond, know is disrupted or chronically ill-maintained, then the other dynamic bonds of trust, reliance, commitment, and touch seem to also become adversely affected, diminishing the overall feeling of closeness and love in your relationship (see figure 7.1).

Figure 7.1

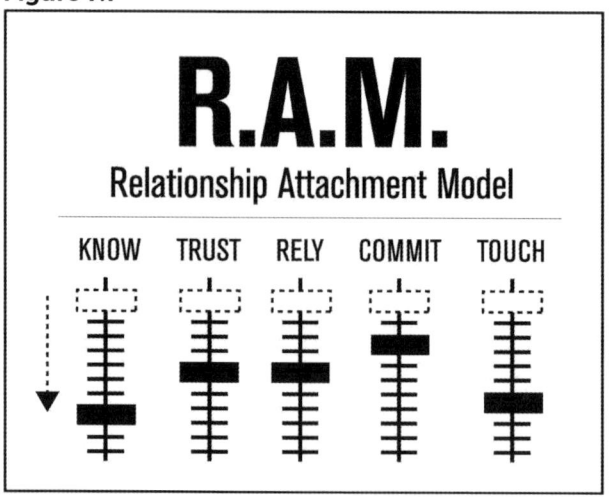

Communication theory became a central area of research beginning around 1960. Most communication theories identified three main components that comprised the act of communication. Although they came to be called by numerous names, essentially, they were the messenger (speaker), the receiver (listener) and the content.

There is a fascinating chapter in the New Testament, 1 Corinthians 8, that captures these three main components of healthy communication in the words and actions of the Christians in the church at Corinth, and provides us with an important balance that takes into account not just the words of the message, but the hearts of the messenger and the receiver.

There is quite a bit of background that needs to be explained if we are to fully understand this passage. There was a conflict in the church at Corinth between the mature Christians who knew their freedoms in Christ, and those who were less mature and who were easily bothered by things associated with their life before Christ. The city of Corinth, like many Roman cities, had a large agora—an open marketplace approximately the size of seven football fields. In this agora were many shops, small idol "temples"—small structures for the worship and communal meals of different Greek religions—political structures including a courtroom and seat for the Judge (called the Bema seat), and community points of interest.

The conflict was over the meat that was sold in the agora at the idol temples. Because there was no refrigeration, an idol temple would sell the meat left over from their animal sacrifice the same day of the ceremony. By evening, any meat unsold would drop in price. Therefore, smart shoppers would purchase their meat from these idol temples in early evening (when the price dropped but there was still some selection). The less mature Christians whom Paul referred to as having weak consciences

> # Communication is much more about motives, meanings, feelings and perception than rote content.

(easily offended) never bought this kind of meat because of its association with idolatry. In fact, they were very offended by those who had always bought meat in this fashion.

Paul refers to three primary components of healthy communication as he navigates through a resolution to their conflict in chapter 8 of 1 Corinthians. First, he deals with the content of the argument (verse 4). Essentially, he points out that the meat is not contaminated because there is no such thing as an idol. Meat is meat, and regardless of where it came from, it cannot be altered by pagan practices. However, later, Paul explained that Christians should not join in with the pagan ceremony and dinner (9:19-22), but that when it comes to buying the meat sold in the marketplace, they do not need to avoid eating or purchasing the meat leftover from any ritual sacrifices (9:25-27).

But Paul cannot discuss the content without addressing the motives and conscience of the messenger. For instance, he explains that if the one who eats the meat (the messenger) actually is unsure in their own conscience of what they are doing, and they feel a bit guilty about their actions, then this act becomes sin to them because they are not honoring their conscience (8:7). This description illustrates the role of the messenger in any act of communication. It is not just the content of what you do or say that matters to God, it is also the intent of your heart and mind. It is vital that the one speaking has enough self-awareness to know what has prompted their words, their inner motives that are wrapped up in their words.

> **Communication becomes complicated because there isn't just one truth.**

The motive of the messenger is also implied in the very first verse where Paul states that *knowledge alone makes one arrogant, but love edifies—encourages, strengthens and builds up another*. In other words, in your relationship, just because you are saying something that is right does not mean that you are being loving! It is not just the content of what you are saying, but it is also the motives of your heart in why you are talking that way.

The final component in any communication is the receiver— the perception of the one listening. This passage does not address the importance of how someone listens (see other passages like James 1:19 for how you should listen), but it does emphasize the ways that the receiver views the messenger and interprets the message. In the case of the Corinthian Christians, there were those who were offended by the actions of the *meat-eaters*. They were lacking knowledge of the freedom they had to eat this kind of meat. However, Paul does not condescend to them by telling them to grow up in their faith. Instead, he holds the *messengers* responsible for how they are coming across to the receivers. The Phillips translation of verses 9 and 12 reads this way, *You must be careful that your freedom to eat meat does not in any way hinder anyone whose faith is not as robust as yours... And when you sin like this and damage the weak consciences of your brethren, you really sin against Christ.*

This is quite a profound passage when you begin to apply it to your marriage relationship. Basically, Paul is saying that even when you are right and are doing nothing wrong, when your words and/ or actions come across to your spouse in ways that are offensive and hurtful, then you must accept some level of responsibility. The perception and interpretation of the receiver is not negated by the innocence of the messenger or the content of their message.

Let me use an example from my own marriage to illustrate these three aspects. It was the summer of 1978, and Shirley and I had been dating for about nine months. We met at college in Philadelphia, and although I had been to her home in Pennsylvania, she had never met my family back in Ohio. She was going to fly out to Cleveland for our July 4th party and meet my parents and the whole clan. Needless to say, she was nervous. Now remember, no cell phones back in those dark ages.

I drove up to the Cleveland airport around 11:00 AM to pick her up. I parked and went into the airport. However, the Delta flight numbers she had given me didn't match any of the arriving flights. I hustled around to the different airlines and checked their incoming flights, thinking that she may have been mistaken about the specific airline she was traveling on. After an hour or so, I headed back to my parent's home, wondering what happened.

Shortly after I arrived home, the phone rang. Shirley was calling from a pay phone in the airport, quite upset and confused because she had arrived, and was waiting for over an hour but I was nowhere to be found. I explained that I had been there, and ran to all the airlines looking for her flight, but could not even find the actual flight she was on. I told her to read to me her ticket, and with some frustration she read,

> Delta... flight 1420... arrival 11:12 AM... Columbus International Airport.
> "Columbus!" I exclaimed. "That is not where you were supposed to come. I had told you, Cleveland."
> What?!? Are you kidding me. I swear that you said, Columbus.

Not what Shirley wanted for her first impression with my family. They all got a chuckle out of her mistaken destination, but not so funny for her down in Columbus. Fortunately, the airline took pity on her and immediately, put her on a puddle-jumper up to Cleveland. But you can imagine the emotional shift of our first conversation together in my home state of Ohio.

Now that we are forty years from this mishap, and emotions have long settled, let me analyze it with the three components of communication. I was the **messenger**, informing Shirley of the details

> **This is why I believe that although you should take full responsibility for whatever you say and do, you should also take some responsibility for how another perceives you. Of course, you cannot control the perception of another; however, you can still acknowledge with sincerity, that you "came across" in a hurtful or an offensive way.**

of her travel plans to come to visit me and my family. Shirley was the receiver, or what you could call the **listener**. And the **content** was what I actually said in our conversations about purchasing her airline tickets.

No one will know for absolute certainty, whether I said Cleveland or Columbus. However, it is most likely that I said Cleveland because, at that time in my life, I had never flown in or out of Columbus, and I wasn't even aware of an airport in Columbus.

But clarifying the content when Shirley was stranded in Columbus brought about little to no comfort under the circumstances. This is because communication is much more about motives, meanings, feelings and perception than rote content. I needed to get into Shirley's world as a young 18-year old sophomore in college who had ventured out to meet her boyfriend's family but landed 150 miles off target, and now felt embarrassed and angry along with all her previous feelings of insecurity and nervousness. She could easily have blamed me for not being more thorough with my instructions. And looking back on the way she made her plans, I should have been more involved. I tried to apologize for "coming across" in a way that was unclear, and to sympathize with her plight. And she quickly overlooked any of the *shoulda, woulda, coulda's,* and gave me the benefit of the doubt that I had been clear, and she had just looked up the wrong city on the map when she ordered her ticket.

But you can imagine the potential in this misunderstanding for igniting an argument. Communication easily becomes complicated because there is not just one truth. There is what *I think I said*; and what *you think I said*; and then there is what I really did say. But then there is also what *I think* about why I said what I did; and what *you think* about why I said what I did; and then there is how *I felt* when I said it and how *you felt* about what you thought I said and why I said it. No wonder the number one problem couples say they experience in their relationships is communication!

There is an old saying, *perception is reality*, and your communication is the perfect example of how true this statement really is.

You could be completely innocent in your motives, and what you said could have been totally accurate, but if you *came across* to your spouse in an offensive way, then your message was received with that hurtful emotion.

Now, I know some who would dismiss their partner's perspective, claiming that they did nothing wrong and it was all in their spouse's head. In fact, I counseled many who would be indignant, stating that they would never apologize unless they were wrong. But here is my suggestion: take full responsibility for your feelings, motives and what you say and do; and take some level of responsibility for how your spouse perceives you.

Most of your conflicts in marriage will be misunderstandings in which you will say one thing while your spouse hears another. Therefore, you need to be very aware of not only what you say, and your feelings and motives, but also the ways that your partner understands you and what you have said!

I think that when your spouse misunderstands you, the natural reaction is to explain what you really meant, or why you did what you did. But an explanation does not always make your spouse feel better. This is what Marvin had to figure out in his communication with Claudia.

> Hey Doc, maybe you can get Marvin to stop yelling at me when he is helping me on the computer, Claudia complained as they walked in for their fourth counseling session.
> "Whaaat?!" Marvin exclaimed.

Claudia stared at him in disbelief. After about seven seconds, she turned to me to explain,

> Marvin has been teaching me how to use a new software program that I use with our home finances. But whenever I don't catch on right away, he yells at me.

I do not! Marvin protested. "Give me an example of when I yelled at you."

"Two nights ago." Claudia continued, "You became frustrated when I could not figure out how to sync the checking account with the program, and you yelled, 'You are doing the steps out of order!'"

"Huh-well, I did say that... but I did not yell!" Marvin said a bit defensively.

> **...you can validate your partner's perspective even when you feel you have unjustifiably been cast in a negative light.**

"Yes, you did. And you make me feel like a little child being scolded by her father."

"I-did-not!" Marvin insisted.

Before I resolve this conflict between Claudia and Marvin, let me give you a bit of the back story on Claudia so that you can understand why she was prone to viewing any criticism as yelling. Claudia grew up as the oldest of four children, and her three younger siblings were boys. Her father was a yeller who thought that all the women in the home should the housework, while boys should do the outside chores, and be allowed to play. It was common for her father to become agitated and to bark out his criticisms. Claudia's mother was fairly quiet, and typically did not retort to her husband's complaints, but rather did what was necessary to restore peace. Claudia vowed to never be a doormat like how she believed her mother to be, and had frequent confrontations with her father. However, he was unwilling to ever admit his criticalness or loud tone with Claudia. Instead, she would usually be punished for arguing back.

You may think that Marvin was misunderstood, and that Claudia's issues are more related to her upbringing than her marriage. And let's assume that you are completely correct. And for this pattern to ever change, this pattern of Claudia viewing her husband as overly critical, then Claudia would have to develop some insight into the ways she projects her father onto her husband. She would have to consciously think through her initial reaction of feeling attacked and try and see her husband's words, behaviors and intentions independent of the association with her father's treatment of her.

However, if Marvin continued to just defend himself, would he not be re-enacting her father's defensiveness and completely invalidating her feelings or perspectives? And anyway, doesn't everyone have some sort of *back story* that influences the filter they use when interpreting another person's words and actions?

In most marriages, there will be more conflicts that result from a misunderstanding of what your spouse said or did, than from intentionally hurtful behaviors. If your only response to being misunderstood is to explain and defend, then eventually your spouse will feel that you are always right, and there is never any validity to their perspective.

So, what does it look like to take some responsibility for how you come across? First, I had Marvin stop trying to convince Claudia that he did not yell, and to listen to what she was saying. Then, he could put into his own words the explanation she gave of how he came across.

"Claudia," Marvin began as he attempted to respond nondefensively and with a measure of responsibility for how he impacted her.

"When we were working together a couple of nights ago, and I was frustrated that you were not following the order that I had suggested for syncing the data, I now know that I came across as angry and yelling at you. Even though I wasn't aware of being so upset, I believe that this is how I came across. I want to apologize for coming across too intensely when you were doing your best to learn this new program. I didn't mean to sound critical and wasn't even aware of feeling mad at you, but still I came across as attacking—so I am really sorry."

Technically, Marvin cannot apologize for yelling or even being overly upset, because he does not believe that he felt that intense, or spoke that loudly, or was motivated by the kind of anger that Claudia perceived. And yet, he can acknowledge that Claudia saw him in that negative light, and he can validate her perspective, accepting that he may have somehow contributed to this without realizing it.

Essentially, the phrase, *how I came across* means the same thing as, *this is how you perceived me.* But rather than using a you-statement, it is stating your spouse's perspective in an I-statement, which emphasizes your own responsibility as the "messenger." Marvin needed to be willing to admit that his view of himself may not be the only view. **This is a universal truth: there are times when all of us come across differently than what we mean to express.**

Claudia was much more willing to consider the influence of her past upbringing on her present reactions to Marvin after he validated her perspective in this way. It took Marvin several times of going through this type of response to Claudia to wrap his head around the phrase, *how I came across.* But in time, he added it to his communication style and found that it was a powerful way to accept some responsibility for how he impacted Claudia, especially when he believed that he had done nothing wrong. And Claudia became more willing to let go of her hurt and to be receptive to Marvin's explanation.

It is true that for Marvin and Claudia to ultimately change this pattern in their communication, Claudia will need to stop viewing Marvin through the lens of her father. But when Marvin was just defending himself and telling Claudia that she was wrong in how she was seeing him, then he was acting more like her father and repeating the script from her childhood. As he changed his reaction, apologizing for how he came across, and validating her perspective, he helped Claudia to break out of her old script and to begin to create a new pattern of communication.

It is important to point out that this approach did not replace Marvin's *defense*. Rather, it couched his explanation within the context of understanding and validating Claudia's feelings and perspective. This approach softened Claudia's anger, and made her much more open to reconsidering her negative view of Marvin as always yelling whenever he felt frustrated or irritated.

Marvin and Claudia are examples of how you can validate your partner's perspective even when you feel you have been unjustifiably cast in a negative light. This approach can also strengthen your communication in less conflictual situations. Restating in your own words your spouse's views, feelings and perspectives will let them know you were genuinely listening. It provides some feedback that will also make sure that what you think your spouse said is really what they meant!

I am not a real big fan of the phrase, *so what I hear you saying...* but I will admit that the idea behind this overused line is very legitimate. Practice putting in your own words what you hear your partner say, and the feelings that you think go along with what they are talking about, and you will see your communication improve dramatically.

A couple of things will be immediately accomplished when you make this a common practice in your communication. First, you will check out your interpretation of what your spouse is saying before you jump to conclusions that may misrepresent what your partner has said. This type of restatement makes sure that you are accurately understanding the content of what was said and also the feelings and thoughts of your spouse. And second, when you capture your spouse's exact feelings with your words, then they will feel understood—like you really *get me*. This is the feeling of being known—and isn't that the ultimate goal of healthy communication.

Chapter 8: Trust: Checking Your Attitude

Trusting your partner is not the same as knowing your partner. Yes, growing in the know and staying in the know is vital to keeping a close bond, and the feeling of intimacy. But the content of what you know about your spouse can increase or decrease your trust.

One example is demonstrated through the research on marital infidelities. In 2009, Zitzman and Butler found that when wives learned that their husbands viewed pornography, their trust in their husbands lowered. This diminished trust then generalized into a global mistrust toward their husbands, and a breakdown of their overall bond with their husbands.[1]

This study demonstrated how trust contributes to the feelings of closeness and security in a relationship, and how a strained trust decreases closeness in the other areas represented in the RAM. However, this study also highlighted the differences between knowing and trusting a partner. When the wives' knowledge of their husbands *increased* by learning of their involvement in porn, their trust *decreased*. Although knowing your spouse is one of the dynamic bonds that contributes to your closeness, **the content of what is known is filtered by what you believe**, and how you configure what you know into an opinion. And it is this opinion of your spouse that determines your level of trust. And unfortunately, sometimes, the more you know, the less you trust.

I am going to define trust a little differently than just the feeling of security and confidence in another. It is true, when you trust someone, you feel safe with that person, like you can be vulnerable, without any risks. However, this feeling of confidence does not come from just what you know, but rather from what you think about what you know. **It is your opinion, your belief about this person that produces your feelings of trust.**

I will call this belief or opinion your trust-picture. Your trust-picture is developed as you take the different pieces of what you know about someone and put them together to form a portrait in your mind of that person, highlighting and focusing on some characteristics over others. This *trust-picture* becomes the lens that colors your expectations and interpretations of a person, as well as your feelings of confidence and trust. Therefore, your trust-picture may or may not be an accurate representation of a person when you do not have a full knowledge, and have *filled-in-the-blanks* with your own assumptions.

> **..this feeling of confidence does not come from just what you know, but rather from what you think about what you know.**

This explains how you can meet someone and get a feeling of trust right away, even though you do not know this person very well. Almost immediately, your mind forms an opinion of who this person is. And based on each detail you learn about this person, you fill-in-the-gaps with characteristics from your own mental databases of associations, ideals and stereotypes as you sketch your trust-picture of them (see figure 8.1).

For instance, let's say you are at a social event, and you begin a conversation with a man. If you find this man to be humorous, then you may associate him with people you like who make you laugh. And then, when you ask what he does for a living and he tells you that he is a pediatrician, you elaborate your trust-picture more by filling in positive characteristics from your stereotypes of pediatri-

Figure 8.1

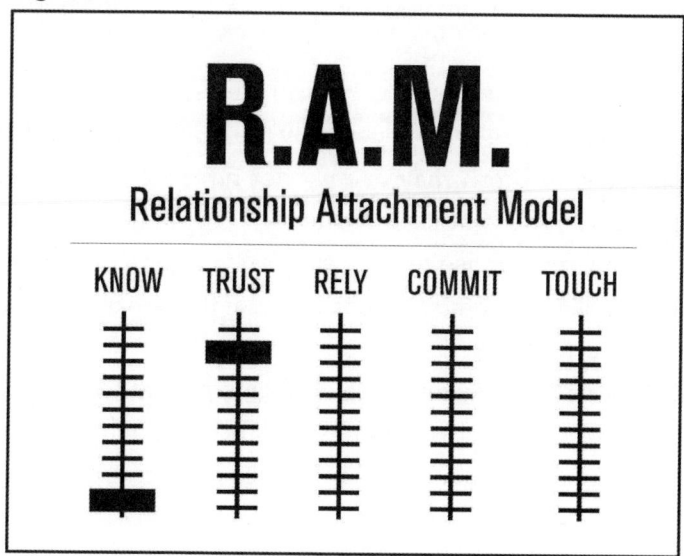

cians: they like children; they are smart; they're caregivers.

He then asks you about your work, and continues to show great interest by asking you numerous questions and being very attentive. This taps into your ideals, and you fill in your trust-picture with more glowing qualities.

Later, when talking with a friend, you relay your enjoyable encounter. You felt comfortable speaking with him, and felt a safe and secure trust after only a twenty-minute conversation.

However, do you really *know* him? Apparently not, because your friend informs you that he lost his license for malpractice because he was selling prescription drugs illegally, and that he does not have joint custody of his children after the divorce because of his bad temper.

Your feelings of trust were generated from the picture you created in your mind, from the mental representation you had formed of that person. You took the bits of information you had learned about him, and put them together to form a portrait of who you believed him to be. And because you did not know him very well, you filled in the missing pieces from your own databases of associations, stereotypes and ideals.

Now it is important to know that our trust-pictures (or what we think about others) are NOT necessarily the same as who those other people really are. You may or *may not* have a trust-picture that accurately portrays the other person.

"But I know my spouse really well!" You contest. "And I certainly don't have to fill in the gaps." This is true. But there is more to understanding the power of your trust picture.

There is a rich theory and research background to this concept of a trust-picture that will further explain how it applies to your relationship in marriage. One of the theories I remember learning in graduate school was called Object Relations Theory. As the infant develops, he forms a mental representation of objects in the outside world. One of the most important is the representation of the child's caregiver, which produces a range of feelings of trust.

However, when an infant first enters the world, he does not have any mental representations for the first few months. This why you can remove something from the hands of an infant, and once it is out of sight... it's out of mind. However, somewhere around the fourth month, an infant begins to retain a mental image of objects, evidenced by facial recognition and the infant crying when a toy is removed.

There was this experiment I remember reading in which a 12-week old infant was placed in a high chair with a circular train track in front of him. A tunnel covered half of the track, so the train was only visible when it travelled around the other half. The infant would watch the train enter the tunnel, and stare at the entrance where the train had disappeared. When the train exited the tunnel, the infant would jerk his head to that side of the track, look startled and return to following the moving train with his eyes.

The theory is that the infant had no representation of the train in his mind, so that when it entered the tunnel, it ceased to exist. When it emerged from the tunnel, the infant was surprised as if it was a different train. The experimenters continued to put infants at one week increments of age in the chair (13-week old, 14-week old, etc.) until they found the age at which the infant continued to track the train as it went through the tunnel, and then showed no surprise when it emerged at the other end. Researchers call this object permanency, because when the train could no longer be physically seen by the infant, he knew it still existed because he retained a "picture" or representation of the train in his mind. The train continued to exist even when out of sight.

The development of mental representations from around 4-5 months old through the first year of life primes infants to play a fun game that is only enjoyable at that time of life: peek-a-boo.

My grandson, Roy has just left that age. But I remember when he first started playing peek-a-boo. I would put my hands over my face and say, "Hey Roy... where's Pa?"

I could see through the cracks between my fingers that he was staring intently, trying to determine where exactly my head had gone. I would then open my hands, and exclaim, "Here I am!"

At this point, Roy would jump, his eyes would become like saucers and his mouth would open wide. He would extend his two arms in front of him as if he were falling, shaking them back and forth. You all have seen this before, right?

Now I ask you, do you know what just happened to little Roy? Well, in a word... trauma!

You see, when I covered up my face, it was as if I decapitated myself. He had no fully developed representation of my head, so he knew something was there, but just could not complete the picture.

Then when I quickly opened my hands and exclaimed, "Peek-a-boo," it was as if my face reappeared out of thin air—shocking!

And like other children, as he settled back down, he would recover with a smile, which we interpreted as a sign that he wanted us to do it again. But if he could talk, he probably would have said, "Pa, please don't cut off your head again!"

But we do it over and over and over. And after dozens of times, Roy would react the exact same way as he did the first time I played the game. The reason why is because in that short time span, he would not have developed the ability to retain an image of my face.

I am exaggerating when I call this "trauma". And in just a few more weeks, the formation of mental representations will have increased, and he will have figured out that there is a face behind the hands. Then, he will be truly entertained. And because his representation is still not fully formed, he will keep enthusiastically anticipating the return of my face.

You could come home to your spouse after being apart all day, and put your hands over your face, and inquire, "Where's my head?"

> **It only takes your spouse to push one of your buttons, and you can instantly rearrange that caricature to shift from an angel to a devil!**

However, don't expect your partner to be entertained. That time of life is over.

What is not over, though, is your ability to form mental representations. For instance, the strength of your confidence in God comes from what you believe about God. However, what you believe about God may or may not be a true representation of God. This is why it is so important to grow in an accurate knowledge of God so that the beliefs you hold about

God actually match who God really is. Ultimately, your trust or confidence in God comes from your *trust-picture* of God—the mental representation you have formed based on what you know about God. It is a common prayer in the Bible that others should grow in a real or true knowledge of God and His will (see Ephesians 1:17-19; Colossians 1:9).

The goal of the Christian walk is to come to know and trust God for who He really is and to correct any distorted views you may have of God. Sometimes Christians can blame God for things, think of God in distorted ways, and expect Him to do what He never promised. These inaccurate trust-pictures of God dramatically affect your feelings of trust and confidence in God. This is why it becomes so important to *be on your guard lest, being carried away by the error of unprincipled men, you fall from you own steadfastness, but grow in the grace and knowledge of our Lord and Savior, Jesus Christ* (2 Peter 3:18-19).

Your relationship with God is a pattern of what your relationship is to be like in marriage. In a similar way that your trust in God flows from what you believe about God, your trust in your spouse will match how you think about your spouse.

In fact, you relate with all people through the lenses of your mental representations of them. And when it comes to your spouse, your mental representation (or what I am calling, your trust-picture) determines much of how you feel and specifically, your feelings of trust.

You find numerous examples of these concepts about trust in both the Old and New Testament. One example occurred with Paul and Barnabas and their differing opinions (or trust-pictures) of John Mark in the book of Acts.

In the missionary journeys described in Acts 13-15, you find an example of two people, Paul and Barnabas forming radically different trust-pictures of a young man, John Mark (also known as Mark) that joined their first journey to provide support and assistance. It is well known that Paul and Barnabas were different personalities.

Paul was a driven, type-A personality who was extremely serious about persevering and finishing what he started. Barnabas, on the other hand, was more of a nurturing caregiver who was moved by the needs of the less fortunate. For instance, it was Barnabas who first stood up for Paul after Paul's salvation experience when the other disciples doubted his sincerity (Acts 9:26-27).

The first missionary journey headed to the city of Paphos and immediately became controversial when they were violently opposed by a false prophet, Bar-Jesus who was deceiving the masses with his magical tricks (Acts 13:4-12). Paul confronts this man and after an apparent heated exchange, ends up cursing him with blindness. Shortly after that, John Mark leaves the missionary journey to return to Jerusalem. At this point there is no explanation, although he may have been a bit overwhelmed by the intense and supernatural exchange in Paphos.

Around a year after this mission had been completed, the Apostle Paul approached Barnabas again and suggested,

Let us go back and visit the believers in all the towns where we preached the word of the Lord and see how they are doing. Barnabas wanted to take John, also called Mark, with them, but Paul did not think it wise to take him, because he had deserted them in Pamphylia and had not continued with them in the work. They had such a sharp disagreement that they parted company. Barnabas took Mark and sailed for Cyprus, but Paul chose Silas and left, commended by the believers to the grace of the Lord (Acts 15:36-40 NIV).

The differing levels of trust each felt in John Mark were indicative of the specific qualities that they focused on in their opinions or trust-pictures of him. Paul focused on Mark's unwillingness to finish the missionary journey in his *trust-picture*. In Paul's mind, John Mark was a quitter. This was in the forefront of how he pictured Mark in his *caricature*, and as a result, he felt no confidence in Mark's ability to handle another assignment.

However, to Barnabas, John Mark was a man of great potential who would be faithful to the end with just a little support and understanding. He focused on Mark's perseverance since leaving the first mission and his willingness to join with them again. Barnabas' opinion and set of expectations might have been influenced by Mark being his cousin (Colossians 4:10).

The intensity of the feelings (verse 39 *sharp disagreement*) generated from their differing trust-pictures illustrate just how powerful that mental representation really is in your relationship. You must accept responsibility for the ways that you arrange the pieces of what you know about your spouse in your mind and construct that caricature—are you bringing their strengths and potential to front and center stage like Barnabas did for Mark? Or, like Paul, are you highlighting their failures and shortcomings so that they overshadow anything positive?

I like this passage because there is no criticism in the Scriptures for either Paul or Barnabas... they each had their justifiable points. You too may have good reason to think negatively of your partner. And, like Paul, your negative trust-picture may have fueled very strong feelings of mistrust. But Barnabas shows us that there is sometimes another way to think about someone who has stumbled. There is a way to look past the failures and focus on the positive and redeemable qualities in your partner.

In fact, Barnabas' belief in John Mark, his strong bond of trust, and his personal investment to journey with John Mark and depart from traveling with Paul proved to be worth it. John Mark stuck with the mission, and years later, was requested by none other than the Apostle Paul to come and help him because, in Paul's words, *he will be my right-hand man* (2 Timothy 4:11 MSG). Paul obviously forgave John Mark; but more importantly, his trust-picture greatly improved, creating feelings of confidence and trust in a man with whom he previously refused to work.

Beware of thinking that trust can never be rebuilt in your marriage relationship. Although it is not some blind leap of faith like jumping blind-folded off a cliff, there is a subjective aspect to how you build and rebuild trust. This is because you can be more like a

Barnabas and see the glass half-full, or a Paul and only see things that are missing. In other words, you must choose how much attention and focus you place on any negative qualities about your spouse, versus those qualities that are positive. Paul exemplified the resilience that there is in healthy relationships when he was willing to let go of past failures, and focus on qualities of strength in Mark.

Although at two different times in John Mark's life, both Barnabas and Paul become role models for you to follow in your marriages. Be like Paul, work to let go of past hurts and remember the qualities you love about your spouse; and be like Barnabas, give your spouse the benefit of the doubt, exaggerate their good qualities in your mind, push back those negative images and magnify the strengths of your spouse.

> # It is normal to periodically shift from a good to bad attitude toward your spouse.

It is safe to say that you have a spouse that lives in your home, and one that lives in your head! And I know that some of you have had longer arguments with the spouse in your head than the one that lives in your home. In fact, aren't those the arguments you most often win?!

It is as if you take all the pieces of what you know about your spouse and arrange them in a caricature in which certain features are brought to the forefront and exaggerated, and other characteristics are moved into the shadows of the background. Hopefully, you have highlighted the best qualities of your spouse so that you see your partner in the best possible light.

It only takes your spouse to push one of your buttons, and you can instantly rearrange that caricature to shift from an angel to a devil! This mental trust-picture of your partner is extremely dynamic, and will produce varying feelings of trust.

As I said earlier, you live with two spouses—the spouse in your home and the spouse in your head! They are not always the same. But the one in your head will certainly be the most influential in your emotional bond of trust. In fact, you can sometimes become stuck in a *bad attitude* of mistrust in which an irritation has festered into a deep resentment that seems to color all you see. At that point, your partner (in the home) may do something wonderful but the partner in your head overshadows reality and distorts the way you perceive and react to your real partner. Trust, then is the **feeling of confidence and security that comes from what you think of your partner, the dynamic caricature that you constructed.**

I clearly remember a time early in our marriage when my trust-picture of Shirley became a bit out of focus and caused me to read a situation completely wrong. We had been married about six years and our firstborn, Morgan was close to turning three. I had just taken a new position in a clinic and Shirley and I had to attend the first social event with the director and staff. However, I only had enough time to leave my office, pick up Shirley and Morgan, drop Morgan off with the sitters and then rush to the restaurant in order to get there on time. I knew that I could escape from my office on time, but I was worried that Shirley would not be ready when I arrived home. To my defense, Shirley was often late during this time of life, and a toddler in diapers was most definitely a contributing factor!

> **Your feelings are not generated from reality as much as from perception.**

I decided to check in with her around lunchtime and see how things were progressing. I couldn't tell her that I was worried, that would be insulting. So, I called...*just see how her day was going*. She told me that she was about to give Morgan a bath, and then she would be getting ready herself. I appreciated the unprompted reassurance.

But it was on the drive home that my most negative caricature of her began to haunt me. I found myself imagining worst case scenarios, wondering what I would say. And before I knew it, I was holding entire conversations with Shirley in my mind. I tried to shake these disturbing images and reassure myself that the real Shirley knows how important this event is and that we simply cannot be late.

As I pulled up our driveway, the front door flew open and Morgan came running towards me, her arms stretched outright, laughing and yelling, "Daddy's home." It was a hallmark moment...except for one thing—she was butt-naked. As I carried her into the house, it was as if life shifted into slow motion. I rounded the corner to find Shirley still in her bathrobe with green mask all over her face. My worst nightmare had come true. In order to not create a scene, I asked what I could do to help her get ready to go. She gave me this puzzled look.

"To the restaurant!" I exclaimed.

She then realized what I was referring to and explained, "They called and moved it to next week—they said they were going to also call you at the office, so I just figured you knew."

I must confess that I did not come clean with

> **There's a trap of believing that all your reactions are directly caused by your spouse's words or actions.**

Shirley that day. I think I said something like, "I knew something happened because you definitely would have been ready!" Not completely true... but sometimes it is better to adjust your attitude on your own.

However, years later I told this story in a presentation overlooking the fact that Shirley was in the audience. Afterwards she came up to me and with a smile she prodded, "Do you have something more to say..." I quickly apologized, and we had a good laugh.

Keeping a good attitude toward your partner—a trust-picture that brings to the forefront your partner's strengths—is vital for maintaining a healthy dose of trust and respect in your relationship. And yet, so many times we over focus on the negatives in our marriage.

This makes me think of Morgan and Jessica when they were very young. Shirley and I introduced two words that we continued to use all through their growing up years: bothers and bummers. Children, like some of us adults, tend to see everything that upsets them as equally bad. They often react to a missing toy with the same level of emotion as a missing person. But some problems are small and momentary, while others are irreversible, with much more importance. We tried to affirm their feelings, while helping them to differentiate between the small and large difficulties in life.

It is the same in marriage. While there are definitely bummers that can disrupt your relationship, many of the things that get under your skin about your spouse are small bothers. I like to call them your pet peeves.

We all have them. True confession. My wife is an amazing coach. One of the qualities I have appreciated about her for our entire marriage is how she naturally coaches me. When I need encouraged, she seems to know just the right words to pick me back up. And if I need motivated, she gives me a pep talk that would light a fire under a NFL team.

I saw this same amazing quality in her when she agreed to become the Cross-Country coach for our local high school. At that time, the team had never had more than a handful of runners. Suffice it to say, ten years later she had 130 kids running cross country. That was a testament to her skill and heart as a coach.

However, there is one time I wish that she would refrain from coaching me, and that is when I am driving. We will be sitting at a red light, engaging in an enjoyable conversation. The light turns green, and before my right foot can move from the brake to the gas, she says... "Go."

I know that this is not a big deal, but yet it feels like a major "bummer" when she does this! I want to say to her, "I know what a green light means."

I admit that I get a bit competitive because when we come up to the next red light, I am only pretending to listen to my wife. All of my concentration is on that red light. I am like a race car driver, waiting for the signal to take off. I have my left foot on the brake, and my right foot on the gas. And as soon as the light turns green, our car screams from 0-60 within seconds.

But this is what happens every time. She stops coaching me for several lights in a row, and I become lulled back into another enjoyable conversation. But then, when I least expect it, I simultaneously see the light turn green and her lips begin to form the letter "G."

At that moment, life shifts into slow motion. My foot is dead weight as I try to maneuver it to the gas pedal; my voice slowly bellows out the word, "Nooooo" as I hear my wife's instruction: "Gooooo."

I am embarrassed even as I write this. How sad is it that I make such a big deal out of such a little thing?

My one consolation is that I think I am not alone, we all do it. In the beginning of this book, I wrote that it is normal to become imbalanced, and that the danger is not getting imbalanced, but staying imbalanced. In a similar way, it may be normal to periodically shift from a good to a bad attitude toward your spouse. But the pivotal question is this: How quickly do you reset your attitude from negative back to positive?

These little bad attitudes can fester for hours, germinating a deeper and more lasting resentment. In my counseling, I found many spouses had become entrenched in a bad attitude toward their partner. So how exactly do I get back to a positive attitude.

Have you ever seen one of those perceptual-shifting pictures? A classic is the old and young women. In one picture, you can identify an old, ugly woman with a big nose and a scarf over her hair. But then the image shifts and a young, beautiful woman looking off into the distance seems to jump off the page. How do you make the image shift between the ugly and the beautiful? This is done by focusing on a specific detail. When your eyes lock into the details on the right side of the page, the image of the old woman appears. But when you look at some of the details on the left side, the picture transforms to the young woman.

Gestalt psychological theory refers to this as *foreground* and *background*. Our minds tend to move just a few things to the front of our concentration, while pushing most everything else into the shadows of the background. It is no different with how you maintain the trust picture of your spouse.

Earlier I referred to this as a caricature, because political cartoonists tend to exaggerate one feature of a politician and bring it to the foreground of their drawing—Lincoln with his long face, Clinton with his big nose, Obama with his ears, and Trump with his huge hair!

When your spouse pushes one of your buttons, your trust-picture shifts everything to the background and blows out of proportion that specific pet peeve. When Shirley would innocently say, "Go," then my mind would instantly rearrange my trust-picture to distort her coaching strength to become a micro-managing annoyance.

Now please understand. Shirley does NOT micro-manage, and I really think that she is not even conscious of uttering that little two-letter word, Go. She is prone to just say whatever she is thinking, and when the light turns green, I believe that she innocently thinks, "go" and it just pops out of her mouth.

But as for me, in that moment, it sparks an immediate surge of irritation and alters my trust-picture of her in a quite unflattering way (to say the least). If this sounds familiar to your experience, then know that the crucial skill for me to master (and perhaps you, too) is to *reverse this process.*

Initially, I worked hard to settle down my annoyance, and then to shift my focus from a negative detail to something positive. This was a very conscious act. It did not feel natural or easy at first. In fact, it felt like I was not being true to my feelings. I caught myself justifying my negative attitude with the well-worn excuse, "I'm just being real here."

But your feelings are not generated from reality as much as from perception. And in this situation, I was looking at Shirley through the lens of a trust-picture that had brought one of my pet peeves to the foreground.

I will admit, it took a lot longer to reverse the process and for me to get back to a positive trust-picture then it did for the pet peeve to completely shift my trust-picture to such a negative caricature. But as I practiced this over and over, several things changed.

First, I caught myself sooner after I had felt that surge of agitation. Then, I noticed that it did not bother me quite as much. I also tried to replace my immediate negative image with a light-hearted reassuring mantra, "I love my coach."

And finally, I began to anticipate it before it even happened. This was not in a resentful way like, "Ugh, here we go again. I know what she is going to say." But rather, I began to anticipate it with a mixture of playfulness, humor and appreciation. It came to represent all the positive ways Shirley encourages me and so many others.

There is a trap of believing that all your reactions are directly caused by your spouse's words or actions. If you become increasingly aware of the spouse that lives in your head, then you will be able to take greater responsibility for your attitudes of trust. You will become empowered to reverse those negative attitudes to positive. And perhaps, you will even be able to reframe some of the pet peeves in a more accepting and less agitating light.

Bottom line: There are some less significant actions and habits that your partner may never change, and you may have to learn to just accept them and see them in the best possible ways.

In the next chapter, we look at how to heal a serious breach of trust. But learning to differentiate the majors from the minors, and becoming skilled at refocusing your trust-picture to highlight your spouse's strengths are essential for keeping your relationship close, as well as the prerequisites for working through the more serious issues that can assault your marriage.

I counseled an elderly woman, Joyce who had recently lost her husband of fifty-three years. She did not have any serious mental health issues, rather, she was working through the grief of missing her husband, Paul and learning to live alone. In one of her sessions, she began to describe a frustration she had with Paul that resulted in some bitter feelings.

"Paul was a quiet, easy-going man," Joyce explained. "And he was a real hard-worker. He would get up in the morning before the crack of dawn, fix his coffee and breakfast, and head out for work before anyone else woke up. I always knew where he sat and read the paper, and exactly what he fixed himself for breakfast because he always left a trail. His dishes stayed on the table or the arm of the couch, the counter had crumbs and coffee stains, and the paper was left right where he sat."

"Now you need to understand that I love to wake up to an organized house. So, before I head off to bed, every night I made my rounds to put everything in order. I never left dishes in the sink, or clothes on the couch, or the kids' toys on the floor. And with four kids, I knew that my days would usually become chaotic, so I wanted to begin every day feeling like I was in control and my world was in order." And then with a bit more irritation in her voice she exclaimed, "Why couldn't he just put the dishes in the dishwasher, fold up the newspaper, and wipe off the counter! Is that too much to ask?!"

"Do you think Paul was being passive-aggressive, like he forgot on purpose?" I queried.

"No," she explained. "I just think he was easily distracted, and although he would sometimes do a bit better after I hounded him to pick up after himself, he seemed to slip back into his predictable pattern of leaving clues of his existence."

There was a long silence, and then she leaned forward, and with a tear in her eye, she softly spoke,

"But now, you know what?"
"What's that?" I asked.
"I would give anything to wake up tomorrow, and come downstairs to a dirty coffee cup sitting on the table, or the newspaper spread out on the couch, or a plate resting on the arm of the couch."

Do you understand what she was saying? Those little pet peeves that had been a constant source of aggravation became the silent reminders of the man she no longer had. Although it was too late by the time she began counseling with me, I am sure that she could have changed her perspective on his idiosyncrasies while he was still living.

You say, "How?" Well, she could have associated his messes with how self-sufficient he was, getting his own breakfast and not ever expecting her to wait on him. Or, at the end of each day, she could have organized the house as a gift to her husband, so that he came down to a perfect world. Or, she could have timed how long she actually put into cleaning up after him—it was probably less than two minutes—and used that time to say a prayer for her hard-working husband. And finally, maybe she could have associated his messes with his easy-going personality that hooked her when she first fell in love.

This is my point. Joyce would have been much better off not trying to forgive Paul every time he left a mess. And not trying to rebuild her faith and trust in him after she scolded him for leaving messes, pleading with him to be more thoughtful of her in his morning routine.

She would have been better off *shifting the meaning* she associated with his messes. You see, there are some things about your spouse that are not really that big of a deal, they are just the bothers, and they are most likely not going to change. But if you are not careful, you can turn bothers into big deals in your mind, and shift your trust-picture so that you lose respect and appreciation for your spouse.

I don't want you to think that this next chapter on forgiveness and rebuilding trust necessarily applies to these types of situations. So, make sure that you separate the bummers from the bothers, and the legitimate breaches of trust from the little morning messes.

Chapter 9: Trust: Healing Broken Promises

I sat across from Duane and Maria as she tearfully described the details of her online relationship that resulted in a secret affair. He never suspected a thing until he walked by an open window and heard her outside, talking on the phone. She said, "I love you too," and he felt the blood drain from his face.

Duane did not confront her at that time. Rather, he gathered intel as if he were an agent in the FBI. He tried to stay objective and un-emotional, but the more he found out, the less he could control the surges of hurt, rage and betrayal. The image of Maria as his loving wife and the committed mother to their three children was shat-tered. And in its place, a deceptive and seductive liar emerged—that was all he could see when he looked at her or even thought of her regardless of any good things she was saying or doing.

When he finally confronted Maria, she could not deny the evi-dence in pictures and videos that he had gathered. She struggled to explain why it ever happened or how she ended up breaking her promises in marriage and her own conscience. And yet, she had continued it until she was confronted, and had not ended because of her own conviction. She begged Duane's forgiveness, promised to end it immediately, and tried to minimize the meaning of her involvement. And when Duane asked why she would say that she loved him, she said it was because he said it to her and she felt ob-ligated.

I counseled Duane and Maria for over two years, and they were able to genuinely heal their relationship. And how they worked to-gether to bring about this healing was complicated, emotional, and definitely involved setbacks and restarts. However, within their ex-perience there is a template that you can follow in your own mar-riage. Hopefully, you will be spared from the deep pain and heart-ache of a major breach of trust like theirs. But know this, there will be times when it will be necessary for you to forgive your spouse and rebuild your trust, regardless of how strong and fortunate you have been in your love and loyalty. None of us are perfect. We all make mistakes; we all have short-comings. And, from time to time, we all disappoint our spouses.

So, what Duane and Maria did to heal their brokenness provides an example of what is involved in forgiving an offense and rebuild-ing trust. Many of the relationship processes that heal a major break-down of trust are the same steps that you will need to take for the smallest infractions. Therefore, this chapter is not about infidelity... **it is about broken promises, unfulfilled needs, financial misman-agement, harsh words, and many other causes of hurt and disap-pointment in your relationship that will require a willingness to forgive, and a rebuilding of the trust and belief in your partner.**

I need to give a couple clarifications before tackling this most serious of topics. First, there are entire books written on this subject and just one chapter will hardly do justice to the expansiveness of all that is involved in healing a breakdown of trust. So please take that into consideration and if you need more help and guidance, then I hope that this chapter will encourage you to read more, seek out good counsel, and renew your commitment to a stronger rela-tionship.

Second, the causes of a strained or broken trust have many unique aspects to them. So even though I am attempting to pro-vide a general approach to rebuilding your trust, I realize that this one-size-fits-all approach must be modified for every situation and every couple. So, the type of offense, the involvement of each partner, the severity of betrayal, the frequency and length of time—all of these aspects will alter the specific details of what a couple must do to move forward in their relationship.

And related to this is the fact that it is difficult (and maybe, even impossible) to work through forgiveness and trust when the offensive action keeps repeating. Maria needed to stop her involvement completely—both in real life interactions and within her own heart—before Duane could ever rebuild his trust. And if she had not stopped, then there would continually have been some new offense that Duane would have to forgive.

Forgiveness
- - - - - - - - -

When you have been hurt by your spouse, or had your trust shaken, forgiveness is the "letting go" of your anger, hurt and resentments. It is like wiping the slate clean. Ultimately, it is your choice to *overlook* a wrong, to say, "I will let go of my pain and anger, accept that this happened, and move on." However, this is usually the conclusion of a long process of working at forgiving. So, it is helpful if you think of forgiveness in the following ways.

> **It may be impossible to work through forgiveness when the offensive action keeps repeating.**

First, forgiveness is a decision. When you think about it, you do not have to forgive your spouse...that is a decision you make. It is an act of your will. And no matter how many times your partner may ask, forgiveness never comes unless you decide to take the step.

On the other hand, even

if your spouse never asks, you can still choose to forgive your partner. An example of this is our Lord Jesus. When He was on the cross, He prayed, *Father, forgive them, for they do not know what they are doing* (Luke 23:34). They were not asking for forgiveness, and most of those He was praying for did not even recognize anything wrong with what they were doing.

No one can stop you from forgiving. In fact, you can still forgive the person who never even asked for your forgiveness. This is because forgiveness is an act of your will and heart. It does not automatically result in reconciliation, nor does it require that the one you forgive to have admitted what they did, or to ever accept your forgiveness. The saying that *forgiveness is a gift* has a deep truth to it. It is never earned, and sometimes not even requested. And when you do forgive, it is always given.

Second, forgiveness is a journey. Once you have made the decision to forgive someone, you are then launched on the journey to fully release your hurt and anger. This does not mean that you ever forget what was said or done, but you do *work through* the emotions. This always requires some time, and the more serious the

> # In many ways, you will have to forgive someone for the same offense over and over before you are able to fully release all your emotions and reactions to being wronged.

hurt, the longer the process.

In many ways, you will have to forgive someone for the same

offense over and over before you are able fully release all your emotion and reactions to being wronged. For instance, let's say when you woke up, you spent some time alone thinking about the wrong that was done to you. You know that you will have to go to work and get on with your day, so you do your best to pray through it, let it go, re-center yourself, and accept what had happened.

As you go through the morning at work, you find yourself getting more into the tasks of your job. It is a nice distraction from the constant feelings and thoughts of your broken trust. But then, as you are driving home, something comes on the radio (a song, a commercial, a conversation) that takes you right back into the raging sea of emotion, and so, you do at the end of your day what you had done at its start— pray and work through your emotions and try to forgive.

And with very serious betrayals of trust, days can turn into months as you journey through the forgiving process. But eventually, if the offense remains in the past and does not continually repeat, you can reach an end to your journey.

So, the third way to understand forgiveness is that there is a destination of having forgiven your spouse. Forgiveness has a culmination point when you decide to finally let something go. You have worked through the emotions and reliving the event enough times that you no longer need or want to bring it up again. Rather, you have now turned a corner and have decided to resist any thoughts about this pain.

This is the final state of true forgiveness—even though you may sometimes be tempted to remember and go back into the hurt and anger, you know that you have worked through the journey of releasing long enough, and you have made the conclusion to let the past go. You have come to a culmination point, and have concluded, *it is finished.*

Rebuilding Trust

The acts of forgiveness and rebuilding trust are not the same. In fact, you can forgive someone even though you never trust them again. And in some situations, this is both the correct and necessary posture to take. In the Scriptures, we are commanded to forgive, we are commanded to pray and hope for others, but nowhere are we told to fully trust someone who has a proven track record of being untrustworthy. The church at Corinth was instructed to withdraw from some members that were unwilling to repent and change their ways (1 Corinthians 5). The Apostle Paul reprimands the church for boasting that they could just overlook these sins and accept the members (verse 6). He explains that if the members would genuinely repent and make a change, then the church should trust them and welcome them back into their fellowship. But until then, they should not give trust and acceptance when it has not been earned.

I found in counseling, that spouses that had been deeply offend-

Figure 9.1

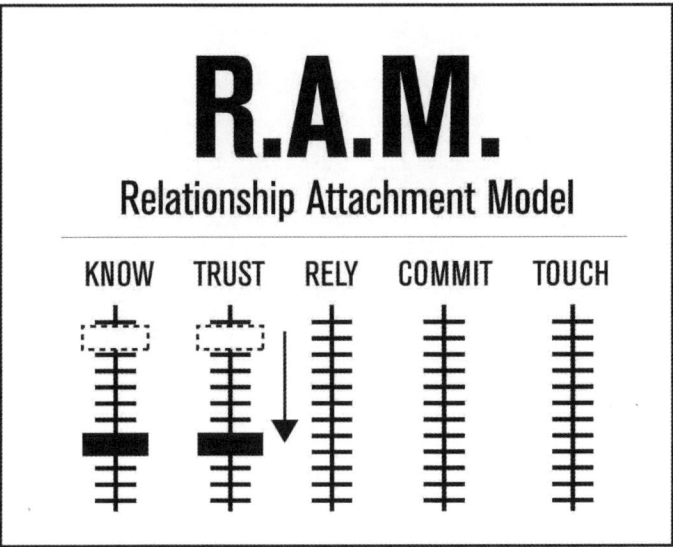

ed often held back forgiveness because they thought that as soon as they forgive their partner, then they would immediately have to fully trust that partner. When I explained that these two processes were related but also very different, and that it is common to reach the destination of forgiveness long before rebuilding a secure trust in one's partner, then they were free to let go of the past while they continued to work on rebuilding their belief in how their partner will act on into the future.

I defined trust in the last chapter as the confidence you feel in your partner based on the ways that you take the pieces of what you know about your partner and arrange them in your mind. Certain characteristics of your partner will be brought to the foreground, and overshadow other characteristics.

If forgiveness is the letting go of the emotions and impact of a past offense, then rebuilding trust is rearranging your trust-picture so that positive qualities are brought to the front, and any short-comings or weaknesses are moved to the back. But this usually requires that your partner increases transparency, so you can gain a reassurance of what are their positive qualities.

The accumulation of new and positive experiences will provide you with the very images to focus on when you are reconstructing your trust-picture. They take time, and without them, you are left to reconstruct your trust solely on past merits. But usually, those past merits have been tainted by your partner's offense(s), so a need to forgive the past must be accompanied with a period of proving that your renewed belief in your partner is justified.

These two relationship processes can take months, and in more serious breaches of trust, forgiving and the rebuilding of faith in your partner can sometimes continue over years. But just as forgiveness has a destination, there needs to be a destination point of rebuilding trust. As you and your partner work together to address the past, make changes in your personal lives, and alter the structure of your relationship in ways to increase transparency and mutual security, then there is hope for both the healing of the past and your closeness in the future.

There are two concerns that I would like to caution the one who broke their partner's trust (for clarity, I will refer to this spouse as the offender). **First, it is likely that you will want to resolve the past**

and "get back to normal" before your spouse is ready.

In my counseling with couples who were attempting to work through severe breaches of trust, this was one of the most common sources of confusion and conflict. Sometimes, it would be clouded in an argument over whether forgiveness had been fully given, with the offender arguing that once forgiven then, as a couple they should be back to normal.

However, I would have to explain to the couple that there is a difference between forgiving the past, and feeling a trust and security with the present and future. Frequently, the offender had to become more patient and understanding of the amount of time that was realistically needed for both the forgiving process and the rebuilding of trust by the partner who had been hurt.

The second concern that I would caution you about is that many times, the offender wants trust to be given without any significant changes in the relationship. This usually ended up being unrealistic with the couples I counseled.

First, trust is built from what you know about your partner. Therefore, when trust is decreased, the need to know your partner increases. Think of the RAM, when trust drops, then so does the know (see figure 9.1). And when the feeling of knowing your partner has been compromised, then the need for transparency is greater.

You can hear the offended partner struggling with, "I thought I knew you, but I guess I really did not. And anyway, what more is there that I don't know about you." If you betrayed the trust of your partner, then know that your spouse will need to know more details about your comings and goings. It is not because you are under the spotlight, or are being interrogated. Rather, it is these disclosures that are necessary for the healing and restoring of trust. Your partner's trust picture of you fragmented, and to become repaired, there is a need for reassuring experiences and facts.

The other change that is often needed for the rebuilding of trust **is some modification in the structure or rules of your relationship.** For instance, if your partner had been mishandling finances, and overspending on credit cards, then it would make sense for the two of you to work out a different arrangement for how you communicate about your finances, what new "rules" are needed to help to align your spending practices, and how you can avoid repeating this in the future.

In my counseling practice of over twenty-five years, I worked with countless couples who made the commitment to journey toward hope of reconciliation. When they genuinely and patiently took the steps to both forgive and rebuild trust, they were able to restore the love, closeness and faith in their relationship. Many even said that they found some greater good that came out of the dark times they faced; a blessing from a curse. I believe that this is how you can go forward with confidence from past struggles, failures and losses. I considered it a privilege to work with many couples who were able to find light out of their darkness, hope out of their confusion, and healing from their pain.

I will assume that most of you are not in the crisis of a broken trust. So, what does all this mean to you? First, practice forgiving and rebuilding your trust when there have been small hurts, frustrations and breaches of faith. I am not talking about those "little morning messes" that just need to be accepted and viewed in a more positive light. I am referring to real offenses, but are much smaller when compared to other more serious betrayals. Your ability to forgive small missteps helps to develop your ability to forgive more severe breaches of trust if that were to ever occur. For many of you, a major breakdown of trust will not assault your relationship. But remember that small leaks can lead to big blowouts. So, make it your goal to become highly skilled at catching those little offenses, apologizing and forgiving each other with sincere meaningfulness, and realigning the trust-picture you have of your partner.

Maintaining a positive belief and attitude of trust in your partner requires that you regularly rearrange that inner picture of your spouse so that their best qualities are front and center, and framed in the most positive and complimentary ways. The more you both do this each and every day, the more your love will grow in mutual appreciation, admiration and respect.

Chapter 10: Rely: Becoming Your Partner's Connoisseur

When you scan the online shelves of Amazon or search for a good book on marriage, most of the best-sellers will be about understanding and meeting the unique needs of your spouse. You will find books about the differences between men and women, the key roles of a husband and wife in marriage, and numerous templates for organizing the personal needs that should be met in a relationship. The reason why there are so many books about this subject is because a crucial area of your relationship is the bond of reliance— how you look to your spouse to meet your needs, and how you give to your spouse to meet theirs.

This area of reliance is the proving ground of trust. When you trust your partner, you believe that they will come through for you in certain ways that you need or want. And because of this trust, you will most likely depend on your spouse to fulfill those expectations. If your spouse fulfills your expectations in the ways that you hoped, then your trust increases, and you feel more confident in your faith in your spouse. However, if your partner lets you down, then you are inclined to question your trust-picture and are likely to realign it to have some negative or untrusting qualities of your spouse become more prominent.

I have spent a couple of chapters explaining the trust-picture, the importance of keeping a positive attitude of trust, and even how to rebuild that trust if your spouse betrayed or hurt you in serious ways. But I want you to see that trust without reliance is wishful

Figure 10.1

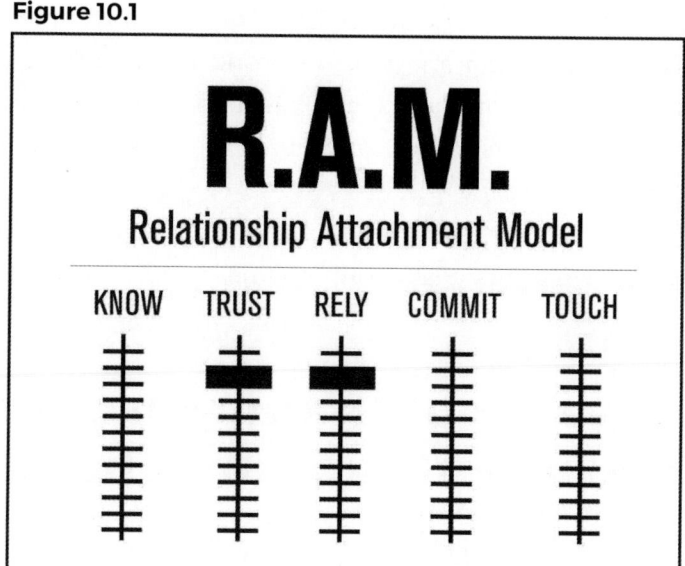

hoping; and reliance without trust is blind dependence. The two are meant to go together, so that your trust is proven out by your spouse's reliability, and the action of your trust is expressed in your own reliance upon your spouse (see figure 10.1).

There are several qualities you need to develop to be able to build a mutual and healthy reliance in your marriage relationship. The first is that you need to become a connoisseur of your spouse. Being your partner's connoisseur is a way to fulfill the golden rule in your marriage: *Do unto others as you would like others to do unto you.*

Now, just to be clear, it does not mean that if you are a football fanatic, and desperately want the Dish All-sports package for your birthday, that you would then turn around and give it as a present to your spouse on their birthday. That is literally doing for them what you would like your partner to do for you.

But, what the golden rule really means is, in the "same spirit" of how you would like your spouse to think of you, relate to you, and love you... make sure you love them like that!

And isn't this the design of true love! For love should move you out of your own world and into the world of the one you love, stretching you to become an expert of their needs and wants so that you can love that person in ways that are the most meaningful to them.

When you are your partner's connoisseur, you know what makes them happy, what they really want and need... and you love them

> # Love should move you out of your own world and into the world of the one you love, stretching you to become an expert of their needs and wants so that you can love that person in ways that are the most meaningful to them.

in those ways. In my work with the military, they called this type of person the SME—Subject Matter Expert. If you knew everything there was to know about a specific area, then you would be considered that area's SME. So, make it your goal to be your spouse's SME.

To be successful as your spouse's SME, you must keep a positive attitude toward all the details you discover about what your spouse needs and wants, especially the ones that are different than yours. When you think of an expert, especially one who is a connoisseur, you don't think of someone who dislikes what they study... rather you think of someone who is an expert in something they LOVE. They can't stop talking about their passion, they understand and appreciate even the smallest nuances—they hold the object of their expertise in awe and wonder.

This is how you should relate with each other. The Apostle Paul wrote to the Philippians about how they should consider the needs and wants of others more than their own, and although he had their church community in mind, you can apply this emphatically to how you relate with each other in your marriage.

> *Live together in harmony, live together in love, as though you had only one mind and one spirit between you. Never act from motives of rivalry or personal vanity, but in humility think more of each other than you do of yourselves. None of you should think only of his own affairs, but should learn to see things from other people's point of view. Let Christ, Himself be your example as to what your attitude should be.* Philippians 2:2-5 (J.B. Phillips translation).

This first step of building a strong and healthy reliance by becoming the connoisseur of your partner can also be explained with the RAM. An expert must have a wealth of knowledge about the subject of their study. In a similar fashion, the degree you know and understand your spouse is a prerequisite to being able to successfully meet their needs. On the RAM, the level of what you know about your spouse sets the ceiling for how much your spouse can rely on you to meet their most meaningful needs. In other words, you can only meet needs when you know specifically what it is that your spouse likes.

When you use the RAM to depict what is going on in your reliance, you should both ask yourselves these key questions: How well am I meeting my partner's needs? And if I am not meeting specific needs, then is it because I do not know what they are (my "know" is low; see figure 10.2)? Or, is it because I have a negative attitude toward those needs (my trust-picture of my partner has become distorted; see figure 10.3)? Or, is it because I am simply unwilling to give to my partner in the ways that are important to them (my commitment has not embraced these specific needs of my partner; see figure 10.4)?

The RAM can help you to understand why a bond in your relationship is lacking, and how that area of your relationship may be impacted by the other bonds. The interaction between the bonds in the RAM portray how there may be different explanations for the same low rating on the reliance scale. In the first example, the reliance is low because the spouse lacks understanding of what their partner needs. However, in the last example, the spouse clearly

Figure 10.2

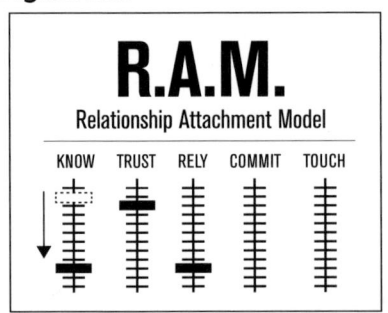

Figure 10.3

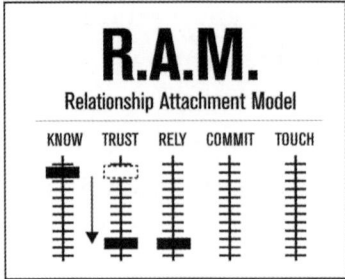

Figure 10.4

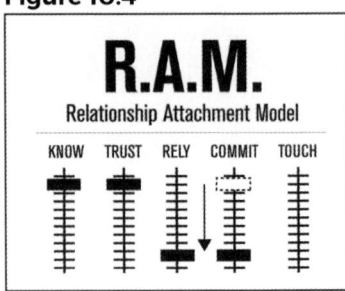

understands what their partner wants, but they have neglected to make those needs a priority. This would not be depicted as a low level on the know scale, but rather a low level on the commitment bond. And as a result, the neglected spouse would struggle to trust their partner to have a high enough commitment to really take their needs seriously.

So, to keep your reliance strong, you need to be a connoisseur who really knows your partner, and this means that you will also have to have a positive trust-picture of your partner and their desires and needs, and that you are committed enough to your partner to make all of this a high priority. Which brings up a second quality necessary for building a strong reliance in your relationship: be an initiator in your relationship.

Relationships don't run themselves. Although your relationship can have some momentum for a while, eventually the good times that fueled your feelings of closeness and connection run dry.

There was an interesting research study with married couples on this subject—they used the label, "relationship manager." The study found that many men were the primary relationship managers during the beginning of dating and continued in this role into their engagement. But the closer the couples drew to their wedding day, the more active the women became with running the relationship, while the men became less involved.

By the time they were married for a year, most men were no longer the initiators of adventures, dates, or times of communication (most only initiated sex). Something is woefully wrong in this picture! [1]

There is a key New Testament passage that provides the most extensive description of the roles and responsibilities of the husband and wife.

Wives, understand and support your husbands in ways that show your support for Christ. The husband provides leadership to his wife the way Christ does to his church, not by domineering but by cherishing. So just as the church submits to Christ as he exercises such leadership, wives should likewise submit to their husbands.

Husbands, go all out in your love for your wives, exactly as Christ did for the church—a love marked by giving, not getting. Christ's love makes the church whole. His words evoke her beauty. Everything he does and says is designed to bring the best out of her, dressing her in dazzling white silk, radiant with holiness. And that is how husbands ought to love their wives. They're really doing themselves a favor—since they're already "one" in marriage.

No one abuses his own body, does he? No, he feeds and pampers it. That's how Christ treats us, the church, since we are part of his body. And this is why a man leaves father and mother and cherishes his wife. No longer two, they become "one flesh." This is a huge mystery, and I don't pretend to understand it all. What is clearest to me is the way Christ treats the church. And this provides a good picture of how each husband is to treat his wife, loving himself in loving her, and how each wife is to honor her husband. Ephesians 5:22-33 (MSG)

At first glance, the charge to wives to submit to their own husbands seems contrary to the way of the world today. However, when we look at the context of this section on marriage we gain a better understanding of what a godly wife and a godly husband look like in everyday life.

First, it is important to keep this passage in historical context. This message about wives and husbands was actually revolutionary in the Roman, Greek, Egyptian and Babylonian societies of that day. Women were seen as secondary citizens with few or no rights. All major cultures viewed women as property or just above the status of a slave--even in the Jewish culture there was a daily prayer where the pious man thanked God for not making him a woman.

The second context to consider is how this passage about marriage flows from the previous passage on being filled with the Spirit. Ephesians 5:18 (NIV) reads, *Do not get drunk on wine, which leads to debauchery. Instead, be filled with the Spirit.* Contrary to being influenced and directed by alcohol, yield to the Spirit of God. Then, verse 21 reads, *Submit to one another out of reverence for Christ.* The idea is that as you are filled with the Spirit of God, yielding to His direction and influence in your life, you will also humbly put the interests and needs of others before you, *submitting to others out of your reverence for Christ.*

When you come to verse 22, the word "submit" is not even in the original Greek wording. Instead, this verse literally reads, "Wives, *to your own husbands* as to the Lord" so that the verb, "submit" is missing and looks back to verse 21. Therefore, verse 22 is a continuation of the theme of being submissive to each other as an evidence of being filled with the Holy Spirit (verses 18-21). The concept is that being filled with the Spirit increases your willingness to genuinely and respectfully yield to the interests, needs and guidance of others. Therefore, what was being asked of wives had just been commanded for both women *and* men in all Christian relationships.

This command, to submit, is not the picture of being a doormat or lacking a voice. In fact, when Peter discussed the role of a wife he used Sarah as the role model of a submissive wife (1 Peter 3:1-6). But when you look back at the ways that she related to her husband Abraham, she was anything but quiet and unassuming. She expressed her dismay to God when told she would become pregnant in her old age, she voiced her wish to Abraham that he should take his handmaid, Hagar, to bear a child, and then she demanded that Hagar and her son Ishmael be removed from the home when she felt her own son, Isaac was being mistreated. In every situation that she made her requests known, Abraham yielded and made the sacrifices to please his wife.

So, what does it mean that the husband is identified as the head of the marriage relationship (*For the husband is the head of the wife as Christ is the head of the church, his body, of which he is the Savior.*

Ephesians 5:23 NIV)? At the time this was written, all major societies believed that the husband was head of the wife in one way or another. However, no society considered that this headship was to be fulfilled by loving your wife with sacrificial grace as is described by Paul in this passage (*Husbands, love your wives, just as Christ loved the church and gave himself up for her.* Ephesians 5:25).

In fact, Paul made the extreme comparison of loving your wife with the same sacrificial spirit and love Christ demonstrated toward us when he went to the cross. And for those who couldn't translate that comparison into married life, Paul used the example of loving your wife in the same ways that you care for and love your own body--*nourishing and cherishing* it (Ephesians 5:29). In other words, this new headship was not about power and authority, but about holding a position of responsibility to **take the lead** in loving sacrifices, attentive nurturance, and the prizing or cherishing of your partner. If someone is to take the first step of sacrifice, then it should be the husband, identifying what his wife needs and making sure he is arranging the priorities of his life to honor and fulfill her desires. Husbands, then, are to be leaders... not in the arena of power, but in taking charge of what will enhance his wife, what will make her feel loved, and what will promote her welfare.

Finally, there is a distinction between the "position" that a husband and wife seem to occupy by the term, *headship* and the "practice" or exercise of that position. The wife's position of yielding to her husband is to be *practiced* in attitudes and actions of respect (verse 33). The husband's position of headship is to be practiced in attitudes and actions of sacrificial love and nurturance. Together you have quite the picture of a supportive and emotionally caring relationship, and although the husband is the leader in taking the first steps of sacrifice and giving, there is a strong emphasis on the importance of mutual need fulfillment.

Brian and Sandra had a great thing going while they were dating, because their lives were simple, and their needs were few. They had not anticipated the changes they would face with the additional roles and responsibilities marriage would bring. It is possible to un-earth a gem during dating who turns into a jerk in marriage.

"If I had known that Brian was going to act like this, then I would have never married him. When we were dating, he was wonderful. We both were working on our gradu-ate degrees and spent most of our time talking, studying together, and escaping from the academic grind with some fun, mindless outings. We were best friends.

I never thought I could meet a man who was so nice, so good-looking, and so intellectually stimulating. We would sit for hours surrounded by a sea of books and pa-pers, pizza boxes, and coffee cups while discussing art (my major) and psychology (his major) and every other topic imaginable. I had visions of spending my life on this island of intimacy.

We married by the end of our first year together and moved into a small apartment that was part of the mar-ried housing for graduate students. We named it our honeymoon tree house, because it was a third-floor apartment that overlooked a huge oak tree. Nothing could have made that year sweeter. I had never felt hap-pier.

Even though that was only three years ago, it seems like another lifetime. We graduated together and bought a small fixer-upper in a suburb outside of the city. I took a teaching position in a community college in our town, and Brian accepted an internship in a downtown clin-ic while pursuing his doctorate. I became pregnant—we called her our housewarming gift—but as guilty as I feel saying this, that seemed to be the start of our downhill spiral.

To be blunt, Brian does nothing to help out, not even the typical stuff a guy would do, like taking out the trash or trimming the hedges. I take care of all of the shopping, meals, housework, chauffeuring, day-care arrangements, and even our social calendar. On top of that, I also mow the lawn, clean the gutters, and have learned how to do basic plumbing and drywall repair.

Brian and I have not been out alone since Amber was born, and I know that if we ever do go out, it will only be because I plan it and make it happen. He doesn't take the initiative for anything. The house is a wreck; he has not completed one project in the two years we have lived there. He's become such a jerk!

He walks in the door, tries to avoid me and Amber, and sneaks off to his study the first chance he gets. I have tried to talk to him about what is most important—our relationship, our family, our home—and he seems to listen, but nothing ever changes.

Frankly, if things don't get better, I am seriously thinking of separating. I do everything anyway."

"Well, that's her story—but she hasn't told you all of the facts— like the stress I am under with my doctoral program and working full-time at my internship, or that I travel an hour every day to get to my job at the clinic and usually go right from the clinic to my classes. Four days a week I don't get home until 9:30 p.m., and then I have homework to finish before I go to bed.

I feel terrible about spending so little time with Amber, but I don't have a choice. Sandra used to understand the pressure of tests and papers, but now she seems to think that I can just blow off my assignments and relax. She is always mad at me. You wonder why I avoid her when I walk in the door? It is because she bombards me with a list of things to do and reasons to feel guilty. I know it sounds weak to hide from my wife, but Sandra makes me feel so inadequate. Her dad had a nine-to-five job, and when he arrived home, he sat down to a hot meal and an evening with the family. Maybe we will have that schedule some day, but we both knew that we would have to make sacrifices over the next few years in order to achieve it. At least I am doing better than my own father who was always drunk and ranting.

> **Polarization occurs when each partner can only see his or her own point in direct opposition to their partner's point.**

Buying this house has been a big mistake. We should have rented an apartment like what we had in grad school. At that time, we just called maintenance with any problem we encountered and they took care of it. But with our house, it is always something—leaky faucets, cracks in the ceiling plaster, electrical outlets that stopped working, and a washer that keeps breaking down. I never have time to work on anything, and Sandra hates me for it.

I don't really want a divorce. But every time I try to talk with Sandra, she becomes vicious, attacking and blaming me for everything. She is the one who is acting like a jerk. She never supports or helps me with any of my responsibilities. Somewhere along the way, I think she stopped loving me. So what am I to do?"

> **...the question is not "Who is right?" Rather, it is, "How do our views fit together?"**

"Why can't you both get what you want?" I prodded. When they floundered and talked around the question, I asked it again—this time more forcibly than the first time.

"You have come to me for counseling, and it is clear that you both have above-average communication skills and intelligence and that you bring to this situation a history of getting along—so figure out some way for both of you to get what you want."

Sandra and Brian were speechless. They looked at me, then at each other, and then back at me. Obviously, they had become convinced that there was no way for both of them to be happy. They had become polarized.

"Listen," I continued, "having a baby will change your life, and buying a house at the same time doubles the stress. You were used to a simple lifestyle with lots of togetherness and little responsibility. But you both have become stuck in a me-first attitude toward marriage."

At this point, Brian and Sandra joined forces to convince me that their relationship was, in fact, hopeless. This is usually a good sign in relationship counseling, because the couple is mobilizing rather than staying paralyzed in their polarization. I took advantage of this by putting a twist on their perspective and sending them back to the glory days of their dating.

> "I have an assignment for you. It is essential that you put serious thought and time into it. Brian, I know that you will say that you already have too many incomplete assignments, but I want you to put this one at the top of your pile this week. What good is your degree if you lose your marriage in the pursuit?
>
> Sandra, I realize your time is also stretched thin, but remember how your parents always made time for each other. This is your chance to squeeze time out of your hectic routine to ultimately improve the quality and perhaps the destiny of your marriage."

When they both nodded in agreement, I then asked them, "How much time can you commit to this assignment during the next seven days?"

Brian thought an hour or two, but I retorted, "You must commit at least five hours over the course of the next seven days. Think about it, you both were arguing with me that your relationship has deteriorated to the point of separating, but when I want you to make a concerted attempt to change specific areas, you act as if it can be accomplished with minimal effort."

To be honest, I think I guilted them into agreeing to set aside an hour a day for the next seven days. If the truth were known, when relationship counseling is unsuccessful, it most often is because one or both of the clients do not put forth enough effort to accomplish the needed changes. So, to seal their deal, I even asked them to sign a contract that they would fulfill this agreement. Then I told them what their assignment was.

> "I want you to pretend that you are back in grad school during that first year of your relationship when you were dating and madly in love. Every day for one hour, I want you to think about that time and, knowing what you now know, write a plan for how you would meet the changing and emerging needs of your partner from that time until now. However, you are not allowed to change any of the facts or events of your life—the timing of your pregnancy, the demands of your doctoral program, or the purchase of your home. Nothing can be altered except the way you made your partner feel loved, fulfilled, supported, and affirmed.

> You must come up with at least ten significant needs that your partner now has and how those needs are different than when you were dating. Your plan must address how those needs came about and what you are going to do to respect and fulfill them."

Both Brian and Sandra scrambled to write down this assignment. It was becoming apparent to them that they would have to work harder at changing this marriage than they had anticipated. In fact, they wondered if the seven hours a week would realistically be enough time.

Try to outdo each other with acts of love.

Before I tell you how Brian and Sandra handled their homework, let me explain the logic behind my assignment. First, the primary problem of Brian and Sandra's relationship was rooted in their dating period. Their marital conflicts were not proof that they did not belong together, that they never were really in love, that they should never have taken the step of marriage, or that they should have lived together first in order to test out their relationship. Rather, they had been naive and shortsighted while dating. They should have discussed their family backgrounds more as well as what they expected in their future roles as both spouses and parents.

Brian was reenacting his role from childhood where he dealt with the conflicts of his family by hiding. His father would drink and rage. So, Brian had learned to blend in with the furniture, be invisible, and always read the mood of the home as he walked through the front door.

Sandra, on the other hand, was feeling more and more alone in the home. She resented Brian's busy schedule and became increasingly critical about his lack of involvement in the routine maintenance and the care of Amber. However, the more emphatic she became, the further he withdrew. She expected Brian to take care of the household projects just like her father had done, even though she knew Brian lacked those skills.

Although it tends to be the norm today to get established first and then marry, it was just a generation or two ago when the norm was reversed—to get married first and then together become established. Many couples of that era reflect affectionately upon those first years when they were poor and in love. It is similar to Grandpa reminiscing about walking five miles to school barefoot in the snow and uphill both ways. "Ahhh," he sighs, "those were the good ol' days."

Sandra and Brian were squandering their "good ol' days" by not working together because they had become polarized. Polarization is the most common form of power struggle in a relationship. It occurs when each partner can only see his or her own point in direct opposition to the partner's point. In counseling, it usually looks like one partner talking while the other continually shakes his or her head "No." When it is the turn of partner number two, the first thing that is said is some version of "Absolutely not." You will never hear a polarized partner summarize or validate the point (or even a portion of the point) that was emphasized by the opposing side.

Polarization was the primary problem with Sandra and Brian's relationship, with the seeds of this power struggle having been planted in the incubator of their dating relationship. When a couple becomes polarized, it is because each has come to believe that his or her needs and perspectives are positioned on an opposite and completely unrelated side to the partner's. Polarization cripples a couple's ability to meet each other's needs. It produces a tunnel vision that focuses only on what one needs and not on what the partner needs. It is based on the unspoken belief that the partner's needs are unrealistic and demanding, and that it is impossible to meet those needs without compromising self-respect and self-fulfillment. **Therefore, each person becomes an advocate for self to the exclusion of the other.**

In contrast, research has found that satisfying relationships are characterized by a simple formula: two people mutually meeting each other's needs. This formula, when activated in a relationship, generates cooperation, support, and feelings of deep fulfillment. In other words, relying on your partner and having your partner rely on you is another colossal source of bonding and connection. Just as with knowing and trusting, relying on someone intertwines vulnerability with security, giving with receiving, sacrifice with needs, and the understanding of a partner with the assertion of self.

The hallmark of a mutual or reciprocal reliance is the belief that meeting the partner's needs meets a need within oneself. It is based on an old theory called dialectics. In Chinese philosophy it is referred to as the yin and the yang. Simply stated, dialectical thinking proposed the idea that opposite poles are actually connected on a continuum and that the two points being argued actually belong together under a larger, encompassing umbrella point. To the dialectical partner, the question is never "Who is right?" Rather, the question is "How do our views fit together?"

Nothing stands independent of its opposite; rather, the two positions have common elements that allow harmonizing and blending. Intimate relationships and especially marriage achieve high levels of mutual satisfaction only when both partners are focused on putting the other person's needs and wants first. Brian's and Sandra's attitudes had deteriorated to the point of only thinking about their resentments toward each other for not helping or being fair.

Polarization cripples a couple's ability to meet each other's needs. **They needed to recognize that a focus on the other person, rather than focusing solely on oneself, would have led to a greater sense of self-fulfillment.** In other words, Sandra's needs were Brian's prescription for his growth and success, and Brian's needs were Sandra's prescription for her growth and success. **Find your life (by centering on yourself) and you will lose it; lose your life (by centering on your partner) and you will find it.**

A study conducted in 1984 confirmed this essential bonding core of two partners putting each other first and striving to meet the other's needs over one's own needs. Researchers interviewed newlyweds individually to gauge the degree of equity or fairness in their relationships. The newlyweds were asked a series of questions about how their partner related to four areas of personal well-being: personal concerns, emotional concerns, day-to-day concerns, and the attitudes toward opportunities gained or lost. These researchers found that the individuals participating in inequitable relationships were distressed. In fact, the more inequitable the relationship, the more distressed these individuals felt. On the other hand, those who were most comfortable in their relationship felt they were receiving exactly what they deserved from their partner—no more and certainly no less. "The best kind of love relationship," the researchers concluded, "seems to be the one in which everyone feels that he or she is getting what they deserve."[2]

So, what happened to Brian and Sandra? I am pleased to tell you that they came back to the next session having done their homework and feeling quite enlightened. First, they revamped their views of their dating relationship. They acknowledged that if they had done even a little of this type of work during that year, then they probably would have handled the changes and stresses much better. They were embarrassed to admit that they never even talked about how they would support each other when foreseeable changes impacted their relationship, like Brian's work and school schedules, their unexpected pregnancy, or even the purchase of a fixer-upper. They assumed their love would guide and protect them through those challenges. Now they see that it was just the opposite. **Love feelings need to be protected during challenging times.**

Sandra thought about ways she could step in and help Brian with his research. She offered to use her break at school to go to the college library and find sources on his paper topics. When she proposed this to him in the session, he lit up with excitement. I had to gently bring them back on track because they became engrossed in brainstorming about his most recent topic and angles they could take to approach this topic. Sandra spontaneously erupted with a surge of energy, commenting that she felt just like she used to feel when they were in grad school together. **I pointed out that her focus on meeting Brian's need actually met a need in her.**

The session became still when Brian quietly took Sandra's hand and apologized for withdrawing into his academic cocoon over the last year. He knew that she needed more of him, but he had fallen into an old rut from childhood. So, he promised to walk in the door and give Sandra and Amber the first hour. He also suggested that they set out a money jar that could be used to hire professionals to finish some of the projects that he didn't feel he could do. He thought he could start packing his own lunch and dinner and then put that savings into the jar.

I asked Brian how he felt with carving time out of his hectic schedule to address some of the needs and wants that Sandra was struggling with. He thought about it for a minute, and then said confidently, "Adequate!"

Both Brian and Sandra continued to unfold their plans for making the other person feel supported and fulfilled. At the end of that session, Sandra exclaimed that she felt like they had just celebrated Christmas. I suggested that a good motto for their relationship would be to try to outdo each other with acts of love.

By the end of their counseling, they had a completely different outlook on their marriage. I reminded them that they had both accused the other of being a jerk. They admitted that they had, in fact, both become jerks in how they became self-absorbed, focusing on their own needs and neglecting the other's. But because both Brian and Sandra decided to take the initiative to actively manage their relationship and focus on meeting each other's needs, their bond of reliance grew. They came to experientially learn that they will gain more by giving than by griping.[3]

The next quality essential to building healthy reliance in your relationship is to learn to play second fiddle. Now this might sound contradictory to the last point I just made, but it really is not. Being a leader, taking the initiative, taking charge to manage your relationship does not mean that you put yourself first. Instead, you actively and aggressively look for ways to *serve your spouse, put your partner first, and honor your partner.*

I like the image of second string. Whenever you hum a song or whistle a tune, I am sure that you follow the melody and not the harmony. In fact, most of us wouldn't even know what song was being played if all we heard was the second-string harmony lines... and that is how it is supposed to be. The one singing harmony or playing second fiddle hits only the notes that enhance and spotlight the lead first string.

This means that you make your spouse feel that they are first in your life, a priority, supported, and that the many things that they do are appreciated, and not invisible. To paraphrase a wise spiritual leader, "The one who is the greatest among you should serve the other." And when both partners adopt this attitude of playing second fiddle, then the bond of their reliance can only grow stronger.

One way to express this attitude of playing second fiddle is to compliment your spouse with more than the following three words: *good, nice, and thanks.* Climb into their world and think about all that they have been doing, and then be descriptive when you talk to them.

And tie their actions in with their heart. It will sound something like what I recently said to my wife, Shirley:

> "Hey, babe, once again, I am so impressed at how quickly you respond to a friend in need. You heard about her diagnosis and before you hung up the phone you were already planning on what soup you wanted to make for her family. You are so thoughtful and compassionate to others in need... and I am so often on the receiving end of the many ways you give—even when my needs are not that great! So, thank you."

Compliments become much more meaningful when they are descriptive, and make the connection between what someone has said or done, and who that person is. In my example, I described what Shirley had done, and then explained how her actions were simply an expression of her compassionate and thoughtful heart. This simple addition to your compliments will guarantee to turn your spouse's head.

A final quality that promotes mutual reliance is when you work to be a team player. I like sports—and I suspect that many of you do too. But think about what makes a championship team—each player excelling in his or her own role while also complimenting the role of the other. In the same way, you need to work hard at being the best in the areas of your own responsibilities while supporting your spouse with theirs.

My oldest daughter's husband has this saying, "Let's get it done— and I will start with doing the hardest things, the stuff no one else wants to do." With that attitude, who can resist joining in to help. He is a leader in stepping into the muck of whatever needs done, and that becomes contagious. He is often the one who disappears and is found doing the dishes, or cleaning the room, or taking out the trash. His actions speak the words, *let me do that for you; or, I have it covered; or, Why don't you just relax while I take care of things.*

So here are the qualities needed to build and rebuild a strong reliance in your marriage relationship: be your partner's connoisseur, know and appreciate their needs and desires; take the initiative to actively meet your partner's needs; provide support to your partner in ways that shine a light on them; and work together like a team so that you both move toward the same goals.

Chapter 11: Rely: Creating Your Top-Ten List

There is a major relationship theory, Social Exchange Theory, and it captures much of what social workers and marriage therapists attempt to accomplish in their work with couples and families. It has been the subject of thousands of research studies, and is the cornerstone of many of the marriage self-help books. Although there is much more to it, a simplistic summary is: You scratch my back and I will scratch yours, and then we both will be happy. Personal satisfaction in a relationship is directly connected with mutual need fulfillment.

You could also describe the major tenet of this theory as a measure of the give and take in a relationship, a cost-benefit analysis of a relationship. Relationship *exchanges* are not always equal or mutual. So, the social exchange theory explains that the feelings you have about your relationship depend on your view of three areas:

1. The balance between what you put into the relationship and what you get out of it.
2. What you believe you deserve to get out of a relationship.
3. And, what you believe are your chances of getting something better.[1]

Although you could interpret this as a self-centered approach to relationship satisfaction, I think it is better to consider this as the reason why it is essential for both partners in a marriage relationship to become the connoisseurs of what makes the other happy, and to be committed to finding ways to creatively meet the needs of their spouse. This attitude of going out of your way to meet the unique needs and wants of your partner produces what social exchange theory would call "reciprocity," and is the primary source of contentment and fulfillment in a relationship.

In the gospel of Luke 9:24, Jesus said, *For whoever wants to save their life will lose it, but whoever loses their life for me will save it.* To be true to the context of this passage, Jesus just finished explaining that he would give His life to suffer and be killed, but that He will be raised on the third day. And if His followers are to fully gain what He has to give, they must also give their lives like He gave—completely and fully.

Now, I know that he was speaking of the cost of discipleship and what it really means to follow Him, but there is a broad principle of relationships imbedded in this admonition, and that is this: **"When your primary goal is to give, you gain. But when your primary goal is to get, you lose."** Therefore, relationship satisfaction as described in the social exchange theory is not to try and convince your spouse to meet all of your needs, but rather for two partners to be wholly committed to fulfilling the other, to know your partner as a connoisseur, to maintain positive attitudes of trust by focusing on the strengths of your partner and looking for the ways that those qualities add to your life, and by putting thought and energy into fulfilling your spouse's needs and desires.

So, let's get practical. To build a mutual and satisfying reliance in your relationship, you will need to have an agreed upon division of responsibilities and roles, and a system for identifying what personal needs have recently been met or not met. I don't mean for this to sound overly managerial, but the reality is that relationships must be actively run, especially when it comes to what you do for each other and with each other.

This will reveal my age, but my mother and father's generation had defined roles and responsibilities. They married and established their family before the sixties challenged many of the social and family norms. So, my father took care of the outside of our home (which was no small task because we lived on a farm), and my mother took care of the inside. I can remember seeing my father working around in the kitchen sometime after my mother passed away, and I teased him that I didn't think he knew how to wash a dish.

My wife and I have had similar roles but with a greater permeability of the lines of responsibility. I like to help her take care of the inside, and she likes to work in our flower gardens and beautifying our landscape. The real question of how you divide up the responsibilities in your relationship comes down to this basic principle: Are our roles different but equal?

As I look back over our twenty-plus years living in a country home in Ohio, I would say that we had different but equal roles. But when we recently built our home in California, Shirley took on the job of laying out the landscape for our new yard.

Having come from Ohio, you can imagine all that she had to learn about the west coast variety of flowers, bushes and trees. We made countless trips to nurseries and read endless pages online.

> **It is normal to wake up one day and realize that these subtle shifts have unbalanced your division of responsibilities.**

I stayed as involved as I could, but she seemed to lap me several times as we raced to understand where and what to plant. She likes to now say, "Every plant and flower placed in this yard was touched by my hand."

And now, she loves to trim, shape and nurture each plant. However, in

California, nothing stops growing! By the time she finishes one section of our yard, the section she had completed previously is already needing some more attention. It has become apparent to me that the balance of work in our yard has shifted from when we lived in Ohio, and Shirley now has the bulk of the responsibilities.

This is how subtle shifts occur and as I described in the chapter, healthy relationships are not balanced relationships, it is normal for you to wake up one day and realize that these subtle shifts have unbalanced your division of responsibilities. This is not a big deal if it lasts a day, or a week, or maybe even a couple of months. But when it becomes the daily grind (and California gardening can definitely become a daily grind), then you need to revisit how you work together and make your shared load more fair and equitable. I plan on doing that with Shirley, just as soon as this book is completed!

A second major area of responsibility that couples need to manage is the raising of their children. This is such a big area—it seems like it deserves a book unto itself!

But to highlight a few important ways to work together, first, you can use the RAM to help you understand the crucial bonds of your relationship with your children. Touch, as defined in an earlier chapter, does not have to be sexual. In fact, many studies have concluded that affectionate and loving touch releases chemicals in the brain and nervous system that contribute to emotional and physical health, as well as feelings of trust, closeness and connection.

Over the course of raising your children, you can use the RAM to gauge times when one or more levels of your relationship bonds drop—like when your *know* goes up, and your *trust* goes down (see figure 11.1). Or, when you realize that the practical aspect of your *commitment* to your children has been overshadowed by your *commitment* to your new job or project. Or, when you see your teenager walk out of their room after being in there for 4 hours, and you wonder, "Do I really know you anymore?"

Second, you can establish a routine of monthly family meetings with a similar format from the RAM as the couple meetings

Figure 11.1

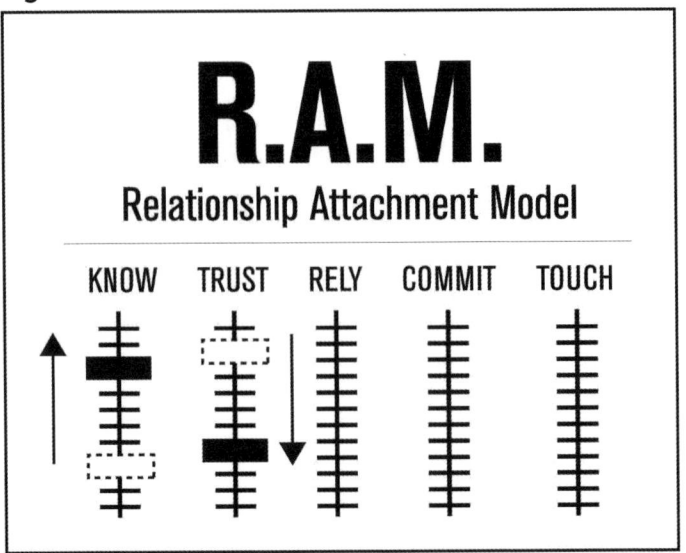

I described in the chapter on Huddles. If you just made a commitment to have regular meetings in your marriage, and also with your family, and in each meeting, you review the major areas of your relationships with the RAM, you would maintain most if not all of your relationship needs. The RAM provides your family with a tool to consider what you are doing well, and what needs to be improved in all the major areas of your relationships.

Finally, there are a multitude of tasks with caring for a child. Be sure to take time to review how you are dividing those tasks between yourselves, and how harmonious you are with working together to handle your children, support them, teach them, and make them feel loved and secure.

Working together, raising your children together, handling your finances together, planning projects together, stepping in to help and support each other—this is how you build a strong sense of reliance in your relationship and meet each other's needs in mutually fulfilling ways.

But marriage is more than just child-rearing, home maintenance and financial planning. There are lots of activities that build intimacy and shared experiences, and meet more personal and relational needs than just survival. I will list ten categories that capture much of what couples do together to enjoy life and their relationship.

These ten areas have been identified in numerous research articles on close relationships and the relationship activities that contribute to feelings of intimacy. I suggest that you talk about the specifics you like in each category, and include these categories as a check list each time you have your couple huddle. This should help you to avoid falling into the "dinner and a movie" rut of a date night.

Romance

Romance comes in many forms, from the simple to the extravagant. A cruise in the Caribbean might be what you think of when you imagine romance. But be careful to not overlook the many small ways to make a big impression. For instance, stealing your spouse away for twenty minutes to watch a majestic sunset, arm-in-arm could be wonderfully romantic, and so could a walk on a moonlit night, or a quiet evening in front of a fireplace, or just sitting on the couch and reminiscing about the good times you have shared. Romance includes surprises, adventures, and experiences and settings that are aesthetically pleasing, that prompt an appreciation of beauty.

Affection and Nurturing

I remember one of my mentors saying that affection often comes with the touch of the hand and the touch of the heart. Learn the types of touch that convey messages of support, encouragement, comfort and love. Also, learn the words that are meaningful to your spouse and that they appreciate hearing you say. Compliments and expressions of appreciation carry a lot more meaning when they are descriptive and not so predictable.

When I reflect on my own family I think this is very true. My parents had a good marriage. They were both quite affectionate with each other. I remember seeing them walk hand in hand or sit and snuggle on a couch. My mother was a caregiver and more verbal and affectionate with her children than was my father. His English and Dutch backgrounds contributed to some of his stereotypical dry humor, hard work, and frugal characteristics. My mother, with some of her family background, was more animated and expressive. My father bought a pleasure farm with the hopes that it would be an adventurous place to raise a family of five. He had many fond childhood memories of spending summers on a farm owned by friends of his family. Growing up during the Depression, he found it a wonderful escape for him from life in the big city.

When I was twelve years old, my mother was diagnosed with cancer. Her struggle lasted two long years. During that time, we watched her slowly go downhill physically, never complaining, but also never talking about death. As obvious as it should have been, I never realized my mother was dying until just a couple of weeks prior to her death. I overheard my brother talking to her in the hospital during a phone call. He said, "Mom, I love you." For some reason it then hit me—Mom was leaving.

She died the first day of my sophomore year of high school. With two sisters married, the third in college, and my brother leaving home to begin his college education, an eerie silence blanketed the large farmhouse. For the first time, my dad and I were more like bachelors than family.

When someone you love dies, there is a definite time and process of grieving. Every member of my family experienced it, although most of us never talked about it. My brother struggled in college, my father started dating within months, and I remember becoming more reflective and independent, radically changing my lifestyle and friends.

During the nine months after my mother died, I longed for a deeper connection with my father. I could not remember anytime when he had said, "I love you." Now do not misunderstand me, I knew he loved me. But I just wanted and needed to hear it. Maybe he had always said it when I was younger, and I had forgotten. Nonetheless, it seemed as if I had never heard from him those powerful three words. I could feel the lingering effects from the hugs of other family members and my mother's voice echoing in my mind, yet my dad was now the only one still with me at home.

I decided that I would make the first step. He was sitting in the living room reading the newspaper. I paced back and forth, carefully planning my words. I would tell him that I love him, and then he would say it back. Maybe I had never said it to him. Someone had to start.

After a long deliberation, I peeked my head into the room. "Dad," I interrupted, "I am going to bed now."

He looked at me over the top of the newspaper. "So good night," I continued, "And, uh, Dad, I love you."

After a pause that seemed to last a lifetime, he awkwardly replied, "Me, too—good night."

I will never forget that night. I went to my bedroom and thought, "Me, too?" What does that mean? I love you and you love yourself, too? Hey, who loves me?

I did not approach him again with those words until my freshman year of college. I had made a strong commitment of faith during my senior year of high school, and this had helped me resolve many of the issues that were in my life at that time. While I was preparing to leave for college, I decided to embrace my dad and say the words, "I love you" each time I left and returned. So, I did!

He would reach out his hand to shake mine, and I would grab it, pull him in for a bear hug, look him in the eye, and say, "Dad, I love you." And he would reply, "Me, too."

You can imagine his chagrin when I would announce I was coming home for a visit. No one likes to be taken out of his or her comfort zone. But I continued my "torture," and slowly he began to say, "I love you, too." That eventually evolved into just "I love you."

Throughout the last fifteen years of his life, I don't think I have ever ended a phone conversation with my dad without hearing him say, "John, I love you," to which I replied, "Me, too." [2]

You may not have come from a family that was very expressive. But you also do not have to just repeat what you experienced growing up. Finding ways to express your love and affection in words fuels the bond of love in your relationship. What was needed when I was just a teen, is a human need that never diminishes. Tell each other, "I love you," frequently. And make sure to say those words at times that are unexpected, not just when you come home or leave. It is vital to have a good blend of affectionate actions and words to keep your feelings of love strong and secure.

Mental Stimulation

Years ago, I was given a Stephen King book, *The Stand* as a birthday present around the time it was first published. Shirley and I were busy with babies and life, so we made a pact to each read one chapter out loud each night when we went to bed. In a very short time, we revised our agreement to include the option of the *reader* to be able to require the *listener* to read the next chapter. You can imagine what happened. Soon, we were reading six or seven chapters a night and staying awake until the wee hours of morning. But that *mentally stimulating* experience has gone down as a hall of fame memory in the annals of our marriage.

There are so many ways to engage in something mentally stimulating that fosters a bond and togetherness. You can watch documentaries, discuss news events, listen to podcasts, watch videos, take classes in-person and online, and join a small group from your place of worship. The list is endless, so make sure you update your plans regularly.

Social Activities

There is an ebb and flow of how you engage in these ten categories of relationship closeness, and what you do with friends and extended family is no exception. I am sure that you have had times when you were nonstop socializing, going from one engagement to the next. But there are also times when you craved doing something with another couple. This craving can even be couple-specific.

"You know, Shirley," I can remember saying, "We haven't seen Ron and Linda for such a long time. Let's figure out a time to get together with them and do something!" Enjoyable times with friends and family build your own intimacy, meeting needs you have both personally and as a couple.

Projects and Tasks

In our early marriage, home renovations were an annual event. In fact, Shirley and I would plan a project around a holiday or a time when family was set to visit so that we had a deadline to our project. I am sure that your tasks and projects seem endless in your marriage too!

But working together can be such a warm source of enjoyment, accomplishment and closeness. One of our favorite times of year in our country home in Ohio was the fall when we would gather sticks and leaves on a burn pile to prepare our yard for winter. We can still close our eyes and catch the smell of autumn.

Openness in Communication

Talking to each other is one of the most important skills and activities in your relationship. So much depends on how you talk, when you talk, and what you talk about. Deepening your communication is what keeps you in the know, shapes your positive attitudes, expresses your support and commitment, and even enhances your romance and sexual relationship.

So, be sure to structure times for your communication—I like to call those your talk times. They may be planned around an activity like walking your dog, or established in a part of your routine like talking over dinner. But having a planned time keeps this crucial area of your relationship regular. And these intentional talks will prompt more spontaneous talks that are equally valuable.

Unstructured Time Together

Another source of intimacy is to periodically make a plan to have no plans. For most of us, life is too hectic, and our calendars are too full to just wait for that day when there is nothing to do. But downtime is such a refreshing and necessary part of being a healthy individual and couple.

In American and most of Western society, the concept of a Sabbath rest has been lost. Stores used to be closed on Sunday, and life seemed to stop. But now, every day runs into the next with no end in sight. In neurobiological studies, downtime is essential for meta-cognitive assimilations—big picture thinking like how you view yourself, your career, your life goals, and creatively problem solve. This is similar to the value that downtime offers your relationship, a reboot of energy, a reconnection of closeness, and an infusion of dreams and plans. Look for ways to be intentional about structuring some unstructured time in your relationship.

Spiritual Activities and Closeness

The RAM can easily depict the connections between you and God, not just the dynamic bonds in your marriage. Practice talking together about your walk with the Lord. Use the RAM to help identify topic areas of your relationship with God, what you are learning (know), how your anxiety has been lessened and your belief has been strengthened (trust), what you are asking God to do for you and what you are asking to do for God (rely), the challenges that you have faced (commitment), and the personal ways that God has touched you, and even the physical ways that you have been blessed by the Lord (touch).

Pray out loud together. Research has found relationship and health benefits for couples who pray together. If you have never done this, try committing to pray together for just 20-30 seconds a day. Come up with a simple prayer structure that you would like to follow, like what you are thankful for, and something you would like to ask for yourself and your spouse. The intimacy of joining your hands and hearts together in prayer has been a source of bonding and stability for countless couples.

And finally, look for opportunities to join with other believers in fellowship. Find a church where you can worship, grow, and serve. Build relationships. Engaging in these spiritual disciplines will take your relationship to greater levels of closeness than ever before, and will provide a constancy in the changing currents of life.

Entertainment and Recreation

Don't forget to have some fun! Shirley and I found that the recreation in our marriage seemed to revolve around the activities of our children while they were growing up. They were very involved in different sports and at one of my daughter's thrilling soccer games, I can remember looking at Shirley and wondering, "So, what are we going to do for fun after they grow up?"

But seriously, over the years that we raised our daughters, we did intentionally plan our own recreation and entertainment to offset all the energy and focus we were giving our kids. Many times, we would be riding home from playing tennis, or having gone to a concert and we remark about how good it felt to do something together, just the two of us. So, especially when you are raising your children, have adventures as a couple that will create your own memories of special experiences together that balance out all that you do for your children.

Sexual Relationship

These ten areas are not in any order. You will find that there are times when one category emerges to the top of your list because you have lost track of it or simply had other responsibilities and activities crowding it out. This can certainly happen with your sexual relationship.

However, sex is not just another need in your life. The bonds of touch and sexual closeness enhance and "embrace" the other bonds described in the RAM. Sexual intimacy instills a feeling of knowing each other, security and trust, belongingness, and fulfillment. But your sexual relationship, like any relationship, does not run itself. You must continue to reflect on how you are doing in this area of intimacy, and look for ways to make each other feel loved and needed.

The top-ten categories of togetherness can be used in your huddles to review what you have recently been doing, and to brainstorm ideas of what you would like to do before your next huddle. Regular and frequent adjustments will assure that your relationship will stay strong, healthy and ultimately, balanced.

Chapter 12: Commit: Choosing Your Lead Dog

Several years ago, I was speaking with a good friend of mine about his dog. He had a beautiful husky that he had bred for years. In fact, his dog had been the lead in dog sled races in the past, and he was always trying to get a pup from his litter that would become another lead dog.

When I asked why a lead dog is so valuable, he explained that the lead dog runs the team. If another dog is slacking, then the lead nips at his heels to get him going; the driver's commands are basically to the lead dog; and the overall direction of the sled is determined by the leader. He then looked at me intently and said, "Lead dogs are extremely committed... a lead dog will not stop running until the driver tells it to stop. In fact, a lead dog will keep running until its heart bursts in its chest."

When you consider the Relationship Attachment Model as a representation of the major bonds of your relationship, you could compare the five bonds of the RAM to the team pulling the sled of your marriage over the terrain of life. And the critical question you must answer is this: which of the five are you going to make the lead dog?

There were many social and religious norms that inevitably made commitment the lead dog in marriage prior to the 1960's. Divorce was strictly prohibited in most religions, and society frowned on those who became divorced. Many couples stayed together when they were facing difficult times in their relationships who today, most likely would divorce. Some of those couples found that by staying together, they were able to either resolve or outlive their problems.

A team of prominent social science researchers identified and interviewed 645 spouses who rated their marriages as unhappy out of a total of 5,232 married adults from data in the National Survey of Families and Households. Five years later, these same adults were interviewed, so that the researchers could compare the outcomes of the different paths that were taken by these unhappy spouses.

Marital conflict and strife takes a toll on psychological well-being. Therefore, you would think that those individuals who were able to step out of their unhappy marriages would then become happy in their own lives. However, the researchers found surprising outcomes that contradicted conventional wisdom, and supported the power of commitment in marriage. Here is a summary of the findings of this five-year research study.

- Unhappily married adults who divorced or separated were no happier, on average, than unhappily married adults who stayed married. Even unhappy spouses who had divorced and remarried were no happier, on average, than unhappy spouses who stayed married. This was true even after controlling for race, age, gender, and income.

- Divorce did not reduce symptoms of depression for unhappily married adults, or raise their self-esteem, or increase their sense of mastery, on average, compared to unhappy spouses who stayed married. This was also true even after controlling for race, age, gender, and income.

- The vast majority of divorces (74 percent) happened to

adults who had been happily married five years previously. In this group, divorce was associated with dramatic declines in happiness and psychological well-being
compared to those who stayed married.

• Unhappy marriages were less common than unhappy
spouses. Three out of four unhappily married adults were
married to someone who was happy with the marriage.

• Staying married did not typically trap unhappy spouses
in violent relationships. Eighty-six percent of unhappily
married adults reported no violence in their relationship
(including 77 percent of unhappy spouses who later divorced or separated). Ninety-three percent of unhappy
spouses who avoided divorce reported no violence in
their marriage five years later.

• Two out of three unhappily married adults who avoided divorce or separation ended up happily married five
years later. Just one out of five of unhappy spouses who
divorced or separated had happily remarried in the same
time period. [1]

The last finding cited from this research is quite thought-pro-
voking...over sixty-five percent of couples who were unhappy but
remained married, reported that they had become happy just five
years later. What changed? Did anything really change, or did their
perspective just change?

The researchers were unable to make absolute conclusions, but
it was interesting that "the most unhappy marriages reported the
most dramatic turnarounds. Among those who rated their marriages as very unhappy, almost eight out of ten who avoided divorce
were happily married five years later." [2]

Divorce has become so common and acceptable, that many couples gave up on their marriages. But if they would have just stuck it out for a while longer, they would have worked through their problems and become happy again.

Some of you may be thinking, "I have thought about divorce now and then." You may not have realized this, but you are in the majority of married people. A more recent study found that over 70% of spouses thought about divorce a few times in the last six months, with 28 percent of married individuals (ages 25–50) reporting that they have had serious thoughts about divorce in the past but are still married, and 88 percent of this group reported that they are *glad* they are still married. In fact, this group of almost 90% idetified themselves as not just the "survivors" in marriage, but the "thrivers" who were very happy in their marriages.[3]

It is unrealistic to not have thoughts of divorce now and then. It is in the tabloids and in the news or media sites every week. It is always in your face. But periodic thoughts about divorce do not mean that you want to divorce, or that you are even unhappy in your marriage. It is just the symptom of living in a divorce culture where it is ultimately up to you to make the intentional choice to put commitment as the lead dog in your relationship.

> ..it is ultimately up to you to put commitment as the lead dog in your relationship.

God's commitment to His people, the nation of Israel, was illustrated in the marriage of Hosea in the Old Testament. The Jewish nation had turned away from their God and established the practice of idolatry and Baal worship. God compares their unfaithfulness with a wife who cheated on her husband. And to make the comparison even more real, God instructed Hosea, the prophet, to marry a woman named Gomer who would cheat on him.

But this graphic portrayal was not so much about the pain God felt from the nation of Israel's unfaithfulness, but the persevering power of God's commitment to His people portrayed by Hosea's faithful patience with his wife, Gomer. The Scriptures described her as initially going out with suitors who would wine and dine her. But as time continued, she found herself lowering her standards until she was homeless and engaging in prostitution.

However, after abandoning her husband and their two children, Hosea found her being sold as a slave to the highest bidder. He purchased her in order to bring her back into his home. There is a touching passage in Hosea 2:14-16 that described how Hosea planned to reconcile her to himself. It is also written as a metaphor of how God intended to draw Israel back to Himself after they had been unfaithful and reached a state of spiritual and national poverty.

> *Therefore, I am now going to allure her; I will lead her into the wilderness and speak tenderly to her. There I will give her back her vineyards, and will make the Valley of Achor a door of hope. There she will respond as in the days of her youth, as in the day she came up out of Egypt. "In that day," declares the LORD, "you will call me my husband, and you will no longer call me my master."*

After twenty-five years of engaging in marital counseling, I know that there are very real complications to reconciling a marriage, especially after an act of infidelity. However, God was trying to make a point about what His love-commitment really means to His people. Even in the worst imaginable unfaithfulness of a spouse, the lead dog of commitment kept pulling the relationship forward. This is how God loves you, stays faithful to you, and perseveres with you even when you wander. What a picture of how your commitment to your spouse should inspire resilience, forgiveness and grace.

In June 1997, Lenawee County, Michigan adopted the first *total-community marriage policy*, requiring divorce to be denied if only one spouse wanted the divorce, unless the spouse could prove physical and mental abuse, alcoholism, desertion or several other grounds. They also made family therapy mandatory in non-contested divorce cases.

The reason this legislation made history is because in the majority of counties and states, divorce can be filed without any requirement of counseling, or any other mandatory waiting period for reconsideration. This highlights the legal ease of getting divorced, and the increased responsibility you, and you alone, have to solidify your commitment.

I recently officiated the wedding of my niece and her now husband. I was struck by how their perspective and feelings about their commitment were so greatly impacted by their ceremony. In my extensive work with singles, it is common to hear them minimize the marriage commitment, like it is just a piece of paper, and as long as you have a commitment in your heart, then there is really no difference.

Although I too, agree with the importance of your heart commitment, I think that most couples (like my niece and her husband) never fully realize the powerful impact of their marriage ceremony until it happens. There is great value in all the preparation and planning of an event like a wedding.

One of the ways that they personized the ceremony was to write their own vows. They took the traditional vows, "for better, for worse, for richer, for poorer, in sickness and in health, until death do us part," and expanded on them with their own promises to each other.

The day that they walked down the aisle, and read to each other the vows they had written, it was clear to all attending that the reality of their lifelong commitment was deeply felt and believed. There is a powerful sealing effect of publicly declaring your promise to make commitment the lead dog on the sled of your marriage, and to persevere through the rough terrains of life.

Tim Keller summarized this persevering power of commitment in your marriage when he wrote:

In any relationship, there will be frightening spells in which your feelings of love dry up. And when that happens you must remember that the essence of marriage is that it is a covenant, a commitment, a promise of future love. So, what do you do? You do the acts of love, despite your lack of feeling. You may not feel tender, sympathetic, and eager to please, but in your actions, you must BE tender, understanding, forgiving and helpful. And, if you do that, as time goes on you will not only get through the dry spells, but they will become less frequent and deep, and you will become more constant in your feelings. This is what can happen if you decide to love. [4]

Chapter 13: Commit: Prioritizing Your Marriage

Beverly Fehr conducted a research study on love and commitment. It was a fairly simple design. She divided a large group of people into two random and equal samples, then had the participants in one sample generate all the words that they associated with love. In the other sample, the participants listed all the words that they associated with commitment. Then Fehr compared the two lists to see how many words about commitment were also used to describe love. She found around two-thirds of the words describing commitment were the same as those that portrayed love.[1]

Much of what we consider true and genuine commitment is also an expression of love. Commitment says, "I will sacrifice for you; I will be loyal and faithful to you; I will look out for you; I will support you; I will take care of you." But can't you also hear these same words from love?

This is certainly true for how God loves us—His commitment to you is at the heart of His love for you. *I'm absolutely convinced that nothing—nothing living or dead, angelic or demonic, today or tomorrow, high or low, thinkable or unthinkable—absolutely nothing can get between us and God's love...* (Romans 8:38-39 MSG). The idea of absolute, unwavering commitment is woven all through the description of God's love.

When we view commitment only as an either/or promise—either you are committed, or you are not, then we fail to see the expansiveness of this dynamic bond. What Fehr's research revealed is that commitment is as multi-sided as love.

Essentially, commitment is the act of your will on behalf of another. This means that your commitment can be measured by the ways that you consciously choose to do something for your spouse. For instance, you can be completely committed to staying faithful to your spouse, but low in your commitment to be supportive to your spouse; or to attend important events of your spouse; or to give up things you want to do, to do things that your spouse wants to do... exercising your will-power to do what will make your spouse feel loved is the very essence of commitment. While it is true that your commitment is a promise or vow, there is also this practical, day-to-day expression of your commitment.

In 2006, I was facilitating my Couple LINKS program with young Army couples stationed in Fort Carson, Colorado. It was toward the end of the day together and we were talking about this crucial aspect of commitment. At each round table, there were seated three or four couples. I asked that they share with their table group some of the most meaningful ways that they carried each other in their hearts during their last two deployments. You will remember that this was a critical time in the Iraqi war, and most of these couples had been separated more months in their marriage then they had been together.

After fifteen minutes, I asked if anyone would be willing to introduce a couple from their table group, and share what they liked about how that couple had expressed their commitment to their partner during a deployed separation.

A wife stood up and said something like this: "I would like to introduce Chris and Evette—they have been married about 8 years and on their last deployment, Chris really wanted Evette to know that he would always be with her, even when on the other side of the world.

So, he put together a calendar of all the birthdays, anniversaries, holidays and special occasions that would occur during his absence. He then called a florist, and arranged for flowers to be delivered on their anniversary, on their daughter's first day of school, and on several other occasions.

He contacted a cleaning crew that would clean the home before and after major events, like their daughter's birthday—he knew Evette would be hosting a big party at their home—and Thanksgiving and other holidays. He also contacted a lawn service and auto service and made similar arrangements. Each vendor was paid in advance, and carefully recorded on his calendar.

He then wrote a letter describing his feelings about missing all of these special times, but that he wanted her to feel his presence and know that, in his heart, he was still right there with her and their daughter."

Well, you can imagine the mood of the room as she retold the ways that this husband expressed his love-commitment—Evette was crying, while the military spouses were jotting down ideas for how they would stay close during their next deployment.

> **Commitment is a powerful bond that unites you and your spouse together in a mysterious blending of heart and soul that supersedes time and space.**

Chris exercised his will-power to plan and arrange for things to be done and given to his wife and children that would be meaningful to them. It would be splitting hairs to try and figure out if his actions were from his love, or from his commitment. It was his love-commitment that sparked his conscious effort to think about his wife and kids, and to figure out what would make them feel his love and presence.

Commitment is a powerful bond that unites you and your spouse together in a mysterious blending of heart and soul that supersedes time and space. Chris may have been on the other side of the planet, but in his heart and mind, he was never apart from the ones he loved. I hate to quote an old country song, but it does capture the core of what a dynamic and vital love-commitment creates in your day-to-day experience: *you were always on my mind.* Commitment prompts you to practice **the presence of your partner.**

The idea, then of *practicing the presence* is how Jesus explained His continued care for His disciples (and all who follow him) after He was no longer physically with Him. It is described in the promises of Christ in John chapter 14, when He explains that after He was gone, then He would send the Holy Spirit to bring back his presence to His disciples, and that they would be in Him, and He would be in the Father. Jesus portrayed His love and Spirit as an inseparable closeness and presence with you that brings peace and security.

> **Find practical ways to cultivate the presence of your partner in ways that honor your spouse as if they were right by your side...**

I will not leave you as orphans; I will come to you. Before long, the world will not see me anymore, but you will see me. Because I live, you also will live. On that day you will realize that I am in my Father, and you are in me, and I am in you.

*All this I have spoken while still with you. But the Advocate,
the Holy Spirit, whom the Father will send in my name, will
teach you all things and will remind you of everything I have
said to you. Peace I leave with you; my peace I give you. I do
not give to you as the world gives. Do not let your hearts be
troubled and do not be afraid. You heard me say, I am going
away but I am coming back to you. (John 14:18-20, 25-28a).*

What is true for how God is always thinking of you, is equally
true for what God wants you to share in your marriage relationship.
There is an invisible and inseparable union you have with your
spouse in your marriage covenant that parallels Christ's relationship with His bride. What a wonderful picture of how you should
express your love-commitment to your spouse in your marriage.

When the Bible uses the union and commitment of a marriage
relationship to portray God's relationship with you, it provides a
window into what God expects from a husband and wife. You are to
practice a commitment that binds you together—a union that neither time nor space could ever separate.

There was a poignant scene in the beloved movie, Forrest Gump,
when Jenny was lying in bed at the end of her terminal illness. Forrest was sitting in the bedroom with her, and she asked him, "Were
you afraid when you were in Viet Nam."

Forrest began his answer by saying yes, but then slipped back
into a more positive memory of how beautiful the sky looked as the
moon peaked around the clouds after a midnight rain. And then, he
trailed off to reminisce about the breath-taking images of running
through the desert at sunrise, and gazing off his shrimp boat as he
watched the sparkles of sunlight dance on the ocean waters during
sunsets. Jenny thoughtfully responded under her breath, "I wish I
could have been there with you." And without a second thought,
Forrest replied, "You were."

Find practical ways to cultivate the presence of your partner in
ways that honor your spouse as if they were right by your side while

you engage in the activities of your life. This exercises your commitment, and strengthens how you carry your partner in your heart when you are apart.

Like the other bonds described in the RAM, your commitment, also can fluctuate. There may be times when your commitment to keep your spouse a priority becomes overshadowed by your other responsibilities and obligations. There maybe other times when you fail to honor your spouse in your heart when apart. There may even be times when you waver in your promises. But even when you are 100% committed to fulfill what you have vowed in your marriage, the practical aspects of your commitment—your priorities, involvements, and sacrifices can fluctuate.

This is why it is necessary to regularly review how your commitment to your spouse compares with all your other commitments. When you think of commitment as only an all-or-nothing vow, you overlook the many ways that your commitment can contribute to your secure and close bond: each time you make a conscious choice to put your spouse first; each time you give up something you want so you can give something more to your partner; each time you practice your partner's presence when separated; and each time you work through a difficult time. This is the kind of commitment that is meant to be the lead dog of marriage.

Chapter 14: Touch: Understanding The Biology of Bonding

On March 25, 2010, Kate and David Ogg rushed to the hospital. Kate knew her twins were in danger as she was giving birth just 27 weeks into her pregnancy. Their daughter Emily, survived the premature birth, but their son Jamie languished — and after 20 minutes of trying to get him to breathe, the doctors pronounced him dead.

After Kate was told Jamie didn't make it, the nurses placed the newborn across Kate's bare chest, so Kate and David could say their goodbyes. Kate immediately instructed David to strip off his shirt and lay down in her bed to sandwich little Jamie between their bare bodies.

> "I wanted to meet him and to hold him and for him to know us," Kate explained. "If he was on his way out of the world, we wanted for him to know who his parents were and to know that we loved him before he died."

Kate and David snuggled Jamie tightly between their chests, whispering soothing words over his tiny, 2lb 3 oz frame. But after about 5 minutes, something unexpected happened—Jaime moved.

When they relayed the good news to their doctor, they were told it was only a reflex, and that Jaime was gone. But Kate and her husband continued to talk and stroke him... and a bit later... he gasped for air. They sent for the doctor, who refused to come back to their room because he believed they were just in denial. But when Kate put a dab of breast milk on her finger, Jamie eagerly accepted it.

After two hours of skin-to-skin contact, Jaime opened his eyes.

Kate and her husband sent for the doctor again, this time persuading him to come by saying they believed he had died and just wanted a few things explained. Kate Ogg told the London Daily Mail that the doctor was in disbelief when he arrived back at the bedside. "He got a stethoscope, listened to Jamie's chest and just kept shaking his head. He said, 'I don't believe it, I don't believe it.'

Jamie is now seven years old, and he and his twin sister are developmentally on track.

The practice that Jamie's mom believes saved his life is called kangaroo care or the skin-to-skin method, and it has been credited with dropping preemie mortality rates from 70% to 30% in the Australian town where it was first practiced.[1]

Loving touch has the power to heal and give life. The power to heal emotions, aloneness, hurts, fears, and even at times, physical threats. Perhaps you remember learning about Harry Harlow and his experiments in the early 1960's where he isolated newborn monkeys and observed how they developed alone without any touch. Severe social and mental disorders emerged as they matured into adulthood. However, when he introduced a terry cloth doll monkey into their cage as a newborn, just that little bit of touch offset many of the harmful effects of their isolation.

It is worth saying again, loving touch has the power to heal and give life. I have counseled many couples who had dug in their heels and become gridlocked in a disagreement. As I worked with them to be more receptive to each other, listening and validating their partner's perspective before dismissing it, I found that these skills worked remarkably better if I had them hold their partner's hand while talking. This was not a *cure-all*, but when combined with improved communication and conflict management skills, it had the powerful effect of softening their tone of voice, increasing eye contact, and stirring more gentle emotions. In a word, touch generated a **bond**.

Kory Floyd, a professor of communication at the University of Arizona, in his study on the health benefits of affection in adult relationships, reviewed the extensive body of research about affection and stated:

> "Scholars and clinicians alike have long considered affection to be among the most fundamental of human needs, and with good reason. Affection is one of the primary communication behaviors contributing to the formation, maintenance, and quality of human relationships. It supports physical health, mental well-being, and academic performance, and mitigates loneliness and depression.
>
> Acknowledging the benefits of affectionate communication quite naturally raises questions about the detriments of affection deprivation. If affection truly is a fundamental human need, as theorists have long proposed, then what consequences are associated with the failure to meet that need? This study examines that question by conceptualizing **affection deprivation** as the longing for more affectionate touch (such as hugging, hand-holding, kissing, and other forms of tactile affection) than one receives". (p.383-384)[2]

Floyd, after studying the effects of what he called *skin hunger*, concluded that those who experienced insufficient amounts of affection were more lonely, depressed, had less social support, experienced more mood and anxiety disorders and less of an inability to interpret and express emotions.

Another study by Gulledge and associates examined the role of affection with relationship satisfaction and found that increased non-sexual physical affection was related to greater satisfaction between partners. Seven types of affectionate touch were included: backrubs/massages, caressing/stroking, cuddling/holding, hugging, holding hands, kissing on the lips, and kissing on the face. All forms of physical affection except holding hands and caressing/stroking were strongly related to the degree of satisfaction participants felt with their relationship and their partner. Although there was no connection between the amount of physical affection and the amount of conflict, they did find that cuddling/holding, kissing on the lips, and hugging were all associated with how **easily** a couple resolved conflicts. Participants believed that the vital role that affection played in their improving relationships was because affection helped them feel more loved and understood, and reinforced their feelings of intimacy.

> **Sex creates personal pleasure, procreates life, but there is a relational impact it has on two people... it generates a bond.**

Researchers concluded that therapists should encourage greater expressions of affection as they help couples with relationship skills, because of the intrinsic value that touch has in facilitating feelings of connection, closeness and bondedness.[3]

Touch is vital to your relationship. But, it is not just non-sexual touch...the reality that both non-sexual *and* sexual touch create and sustain your bond of intimacy is overwhelmingly supported in psychological and biological research.

There is a New Testament passage of Scripture that clearly and concisely expresses God's design for sex—1 Corinthians 6:16-18 and the Message paraphrase really captures the true meaning of this passage.

There's more to sex than mere skin on skin. Sex is as much spiritual mystery as physical fact. As written in Scripture, The two become one. Since we want to become spiritually one with the Lord, we must not pursue the kind of sex that avoids commitment and intimacy, leaving us more lonely than ever—the kind of sex that can never become one. There is a sense in which sexual sins are different from all others. In sexual sin, we violate the sacredness of our own bodies, these bodies that were made for God-given and God-modeled love, for becoming one with another.

Do you hear what God's design for sex really is? You could call this, a theology of sex. Here it is: sexual touch is designed by God to generate a bond of oneness and intimacy between a husband and wife.

We are brainwashed to believe that the number one purpose of sex is pleasure. But God tells us very plainly the number one purpose is bonding—within a context of relationship, and specifically, marriage. We are inundated with messages about sex that are misleading—from television shows, to HBO, Netflix and Showtime series, to just about every magazine rack you encounter. In so much of our contemporary culture, sex is portrayed as being all-about personal pleasure, and not so much about bonding with another. But what is captured in the RAM is true in the science of touch, you cannot separate sexual touch from the other relationship bonds of knowing, trusting, relying and committing to another.

Yes—sex provides personal pleasure. Yes—sex procreates life. But there is a relational impact that sex has on two people, it generates a bond. The first and often quoted reference in the Bible back in Genesis chapter 2, verse 24 is that, *the two become one,* validating that sex generates a bond of intimacy and oneness between a husband and wife. It is not just the Scriptures and psychological studies that have provided proof for the bonding power of sex. There is a biology behind this theology.

Let me briefly describe what happens in your brains during the sexual act. **Three primary chemicals naturally flood your brains when you experience sexual arousal: dopamine, vasopressin, and oxytocin.**

Dopamine is a neurotransmitter that is considered the pleasure molecule because when your brain naturally produces larger amounts during the sexual act, it creates feelings of excitement and euphoria. It is also the addiction molecule that is artificially pumped through your brain from illegal drugs like ecstasy. But in a very natural way, when sex generates dopamine, it contributes to your relationship bond because it causes you to crave your partner—to feel attached, a little bit *hooked* on your spouse.

Now vasopressin is also a bonding chemical that floods the brain during the sexual act, and because it interacts with testosterone, it has a bigger effect on men than women. It has been dubbed the monogamy-molecule because in the research studies with animals that mate for life, the males will stop being faithful to their partners when researchers suppress the production of vasopressin. In fact, in one study with a type of prairie dog called the meadow vole, known for *not* mating for life—researchers injected high levels of vasopressin and found that many began to become more attached and faithful to just one partner.

Researchers from the National Institute of Mental Health had conducted a previous experiment on prairie voles that is now considered classic. These animals are known for forming pair-bonds, intense and exclusive attachments to a mate, as well as becoming aggressive toward strangers who threaten their relationship or territory.

Researchers wanted to determine the effects of vasopressin versus oxytocin, so the male prairie voles were injected with an antagonist, a chemical that binds to receptors and would block the functioning of either the oxytocin or vasopressin, depending on which antagonist they used.

They found that blocking the prairie vole's oxytocin receptors with an antagonist had no effect on the intensity of pair-bonding or the protective behavior of the males. However, male prairie voles injected with the vasopressin antagonist failed to exhibit aggression to defend their female partners, and no longer stayed exclusive with their mate. Pair-bonding ceased as the males spent less time with the original mate as they pursued new partners.

Interestingly, when researchers replenished the vasopressin to these male prairie voles, the effects were reversed; they became aggressive toward other males and preferred to spend time with their partner than with strangers. It's almost as if they fell back in love with their original partner![4]

Just wait until the pharmaceutical companies figure out how to package that in a pill! Can't you imagine a wife slipping it into her husband's morning coffee?

> "Here honey, have another cup of coffee."
> "OK—but it is kind of bitter." He complains.
> "Just drink it!" She demands.

But until then, know that sexual touch activates this hormone in your brains, and produces feelings of belonging and exclusivity, particularly in males. It is the science behind the lyrics of an old rock song, "Addicted to Love." But to be a bit more accurate, the title should be revised to, "addicted to *your* love."

And then there is oxytocin. This neuropeptide has received a lot of attention with both sexual and non-sexual touch. In fact, the research studies on affection and hugging that I previously explained cited the increased production of oxytocin as one of the primary contributors to the greater feelings of warmth and closeness.

Oxytocin research can be dated back to studies on pregnancy and child birth, and was part of the body of research that changed birthing procedures across the country. If you have ever watched an old black and white movie in which a woman was going to have a baby—you would have seen her go into a sterile surgery room with doctors in white coats and masks, and as soon as the baby was born, the obstetrician would cut the umbilical cord and whisk the newborn away. And then hours later, the mother, usually in her bathrobe, and father walked down the hospital hall and came to a large window of a newborn nursery where they peered in, searching for their baby.

But studies found that as a woman gives birth, her brain is flooded with eight to ten times the normal amount of oxytocin. This chemical not only aids her in the birthing process, it puts her in a biological state to bond. Researchers discovered in five-year longitudinal studies that when they placed the newborn on her chest and there was skin-to-skin touch, a bond developed that lowered the likelihood of post-partum depression, increased positive interactions between the mother and child, and resulted in developmental gains for the child.

So now, unless an emergency occurs, babies are placed right on mom's chest after birth. The woman's brain is programmed to offset the pain of childbirth, and to become mobilized to form an intense bond, a bond that seems to last for years.

And here is the thing—and this is so significant. A woman's brain produces similar amounts of oxytocin during the sexual act. And in sex, a man's brain also floods with oxytocin, although not quite as much as a woman. But do you see what all this means: Your brain naturally conditions you to bond with your partner during sexual interactions. This is clearly the biology behind the theology that during the sexual act, the two become one.

Sex is sacred. It ushers humans into the divine role of procreating life. It floods our experience with some of the most intense and pleasurable feelings imaginable. But most importantly, it activates a bond that God intended to enrich the most committed of relationships, marriage. It is within the safe and secure covenant of two lives wholly given to each other, that the act of sex fulfills its true meaning.

This is why touch is included in the RAM—it is clearly one of the major bonds or connections that comprise your relationships. Touch, all types—affectionate, friendly, loving and sexual—contribute to your feelings of closeness, generating and rekindling your bond. There are many ways that your physical relationship can be disrupted, just like the other four bonds in the RAM. But when you include a time in your huddles to reflect on your affection and sexual intimacy, then you can make small adjustments to ensure that you keep a growing and mutually fulfilling relationship.

Chapter 15: Touch: Building a Mutually Fulfilling Sex Life

I have a relationship program that is used in many high school settings, and presents the RAM as a framework for understanding dating relationships. Something that has become very apparent over the last couple of decades is that most secular sexual education portrays sex as a natural, biological drive that could have negative consequences, so students need to master it like any other skill, and be responsible.

However, what my program teaches is that sexual arousal and touch cannot be legitimately severed from other relationship bonds; that it is one of the most powerful relationship bonds, and needs to be understood in the context of the other bonds, like commitment, trust and a proven reliability. This is not only congruent with psychological and biological studies on sexual touch, but with the Scriptures.

Therefore, whenever you have a struggle in your sexual relationship, you should first review how you are doing in each of the other four relationship bonds portrayed in the RAM. Many times, the sexual relationship is negatively impacted by poor communication (know), unresolved issues (trust), or unmet needs in other meaningful areas of your relationship (rely and commitment). All five areas of the RAM are inter-related, and when one drops, it usually will negatively impact one or more of the others. This is particularly true of your sexual closeness (Figure 15.1).

Figure 15.1

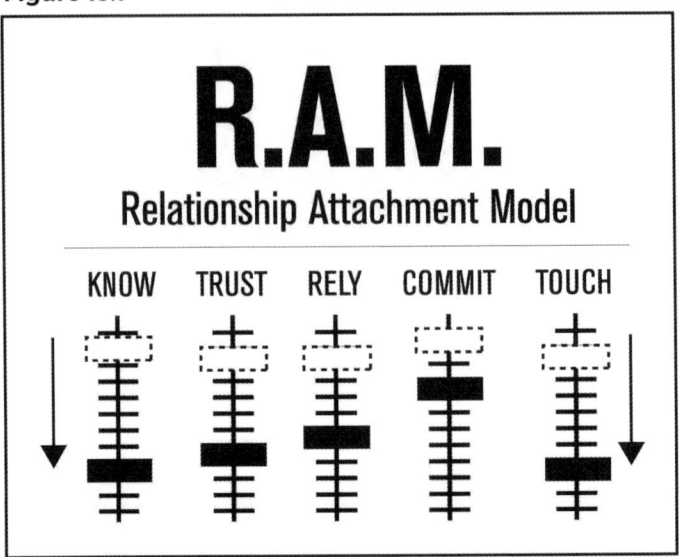

The opposite also is true, that increasing the bonds of know, trust, rely and commit often create a greater openness and interest in sexual intimacy. Thus, the old adage, "sex begins in the kitchen." Numerous wives have perceived their husbands as quite sexy when their husbands went out of their way to help and support them. In the language of the RAM, you would say, "When you spend quality time with me; or, when you initiate helping me; or when you want to relax and talk with me—it is these times that I feel close and in sync with you, and sexually desire you more."

The idea that a person can have meaningless and non-relational sex contradicts the body of science I reviewed in the previous chapter. Sex is relational, and if for no other reason, then because of the chemicals it activates in the brain that generate feelings of bond. But the reality is that sex bonds you not just physically, but also emotionally and spiritually!

Like the bonding dynamic of rely, your sexual relationship functions best by the principle of mutuality. Mutuality was the principle of how you can best meet each other's needs, and work to be the connoisseur of your partner. And your sexual needs and wants are no different. When both spouses are genuinely focused on what will make the other feel sexually satisfied and fulfilled, then a mutuality emerges that, in the end, fulfills yourself. Through giving, you ultimately gain.

There actually is a detailed explanation in the Bible for how a married couple should cultivate their sexual relationship. Paul writes to the Corinthian believers about some questions they were asking, and the first question was about sex. The Message paraphrase of 1Corinthians 7:1-4 again captures in contemporary language the true meaning of what Paul wrote in his answer to their first question.

Now, getting down to the questions you asked in your letter to me. First, is it a good thing to have sexual relations? Certainly—but only within a certain context. It's good for a man to have a wife, and for a woman to have a husband. Sexual drives are strong, but marriage is strong enough to contain them and provide for a balanced and fulfilling sexual life in a world of sexual disorder. The

> **A valuable and somewhat easy place for you two to begin to talk about sex is to describe the differences between your sex drives.**

marriage bed must be a place of mutuality—the husband seeking to satisfy his wife, the wife seeking to satisfy her husband. Marriage is not a place to stand up for your rights. Marriage is a decision to serve the other, whether in bed or out.

The key word here is **mutuality**—sex is about giving, about meeting the needs of your spouse. Sex can be selfish, dangerous and potentially abusive if there is no mutuality. A guiding rule of thumb is that all that is done in your sexual relationship should be mutually agreed upon and not physically harmful to either partner. But within those broad parameters, your sexual adventures and intimacy is to be mutually enjoyed and fulfilling.

Now, this may seem obvious, but it is vital that you have open communication about your sexual relationship. It is highly unlikely that you will develop mutuality in this area if you never talk about it. However, many couples struggle with their sexual relationship, and if they do not make progress after numerous times of talking, the tendency is for one or both to shut down.

A valuable and somewhat easy place for you two to begin is to talk about sex is to describe the differences between your sex drives. The vast majority of married couples **do not** have the same sex drive. And this is probably the reason that for decades, surveys have found that the number one sexual conflict in marriage is frequency.

One study concluded that a low sex drive is the most frequent issue that couples present to sex therapists. And let's be careful to not get locked into the stereotype that all men have higher drives than all women... not true. Many men won't openly discuss their low drive because they feel that being disinterested in sex makes them less a man.

You can try and describe your sex drive on a number scale, with the higher numbers representing a stronger drive. Or, you can describe your drive by the frequency you would like to engage in sexual activity.

But if a *shut down* is true for you in your marriage, then just begin by mutually agreeing to reverse the silence. And talking about your own drive and how it is similar or different to your spouse's drive is a good place to restart the conversation. Even if you are comfortable talking together about sex, this will be a great place to begin to explore how you have developed a mutually satisfying sexual relationship.

Laura and Tim sat down on either side of my couch during their first counseling appointment with me. When I asked what concerns they would like to discuss in the session, Laura quickly piped up, "We never have sex."

Tim cringed but remained silent.

> "Tim doesn't ever seem to want to make love—I don't know if he is into porn, or having an affair, or just not into me. But this situation is driving me crazy."

When I looked at Tim, he explained,

> "No, I am not into porn; and no, I am not having an affair; and yes, I am still into you. But I have explained to you a million times, my job is stressful and now I am on second shift, and we are hardly ever together. So, it only makes sense that we are not going to have sex like we did when we were first married."

There are so many things in both one's personal life as well as a couple's relationship that can impact the sexual relationship. So, I took several sessions to explore Tim and Laura's history, their life situations and personal concerns.

Both concurred that Laura had always had the stronger drive. But as their three children entered preschool and elementary school, and after Tim was moved to second shift on his job, the last two years have seemed to strangle the life out of their lovemaking.

> "I think it was the busyness of our three kids, and then

my job made me change to second shift, so I am not getting home until around midnight." Tim said.

"But then you get something to eat, sit in front of the TV and fall asleep, and don't come up to bed until 2:00 or 3:00 AM! I think you are avoiding me." Laura exclaimed.

"No, I am just coming down from work, and I don't mean to fall asleep, but it happens." Tim explained.

This situation is an example of what I have referred to as **the slow leak that can lead to either a flat relationship, or a big blowout.** Their sex life did not change overnight. It took months. And each time they tried to talk about improving their time together, discussions lead to defensiveness, which led to angry accusations, which led to shut downs. They were at the point of experiencing the "flat" relationship, and it was only a matter of time before some crisis would shake their commitment and trust.

"Tim, I was wondering, when you engage in lovemaking, do you experience arousal, and do you enjoy it." I asked.

"Yes," Tim quickly replied. "Nothing is wrong with my equipment. I am just tired and not really interested when I go to bed. And then, in the morning, Laura heads off to work so that by the time I wake up, she is gone. So, I don't see any easy solution unless I can get my supervisor to change my shift."

"OK, I see your dilemma." I paused, and then asked, "So, if you had to choose one time—night or morning—which would be a better time for you to engage in lovemaking?"

Tim thought for a moment.

"I think the nighttime because I can always sleep in a bit more in the morning."

"How about you?" I asked Laura.

"Any time is fine with me. I would be happy with both night and morning, but if he would wake me up when he comes to bed and we could have some time right then making love... well, that would be great. But when he comes to bed he is like a Ninja—totally quiet so as to not wake me up."

"I am just trying to be nice and not a jerk." He defended.

"Well, if you really want to be nice then wake me up!" Laura commanded.

This counseling case of Tim and Laura have a number of commonly expressed complaints when there are differences between sex drives. Tim, who had a lower drive than Laura, cast Laura in the role of always pushing for sex. He also viewed the sexual act as more of a physical activity that he often lacked energy or interest in performing.

Laura, on the other hand, had a stronger sex drive and felt hurt, neglected and emotionally distant because of their lack of involvement. Like most higher drive partners, female or male, sex was experienced as a source of closeness and emotional connection. And the less frequent their sexual activity, the colder and more distant she became.

In my counseling, I found that these same reactions happened to lower and higher drive partners, regardless of whether they were male or female. In other words, it was the strength of the drive that predicted the behavior more than the sex of the partner.

I affirmed Tim and Laura for agreeing to come to my office to talk about their sexual relationship. Too many couples do not take this step, and they remain shut down. I also reassured them that many couples have hit the wall in their sexual relationship. But when these couples found a way to talk more openly and less defensively, and when they gained some new information, and worked together, that they then regained the closeness that they had lost sexually.

The next steps are what really helped Tim and Laura to reconsider their sexual stalemate, and make some changes to rekindle their closeness.

Step One: Renew your commitment to fulfilling your spouse.

Tim and Laura had lost sight of a mutual fulfillment goal in their sexual relationship. They were less concerned about how give to their partner to make their partner feel loved and fulfilled, and more concerned with how they wanted their partner to treat them. There is a healthy perspective that your body belongs to your spouse, and their body belongs to you. The idea that this gives you some sense of entitlement, or some right to make demands, is a twisted way of thinking about this act of love. Sex is not about taking; but rather it is about giving. When you made your vows during your marriage ceremony, you gave yourself in love to your spouse and your body as a gift. There is a security of lovingly belonging to each other, and knowing that your spouse does not just live for himself or herself, but now lives for you.

Step Two: Take ownership of the nonsexual needs of your spouse.

Belonging to each other, and seeking mutual fulfillment means that each of you must take an ownership of the needs of your partner, and have a commitment to meeting those needs. This can be challenging, especially when your sex drive is different than your spouse's.

If your drive is higher than your partner's, then your greatest challenge may be to take a joint ownership of the nonsexual needs of your spouse. In other words, **don't always be looking for the green light**.

Instead, become your spouse's connoisseur and find creative ways to lovingly and genuinely meet your partner's nonsexual needs and wants. This was what I described in the chapters on "rely" and what is meant by the Message's paraphrase of 1 Corinthians 7:4, *Marriage is a decision to serve the other.*

I once heard a wife complain that her *over-sexed* husband walked into the kitchen just as she was completing a masterpiece of a meal, with candles on the table and his favorite dishes. Their two preschoolers were patiently waiting in their dining room chairs as she turned out the kitchen lights to enjoy the ambiance of their dimly light, romantic dinner. Her husband came up behind her and put his arms lovingly around her. She smiled, and with a small gesture of reassurance, she gently pressed her backside into him and swayed back and forth, in a 3-second dance.

Before he let go of her, he whispered in her ear, "Now?"

"Now what?" She whispered back.

"You know, do you want to fool around now?"

As she stepped out of his embrace, and turned around to square off, face-to-face, she snapped,

"Are you serious! I just finished cooking your favorite meal for two hours. The table is set, the candles are lit, and the kids—they are sitting ready to eat."

"Well," he explained, "Eating is something they could do while, you know, we have a quickie."

"This is why I am hesitant to even touch my husband!"
She insisted. "Because he interprets every form of touch
as a come-on, and he never just hugs, or snuggles, or
flirts."

When you have a fairly high sex drive, you will have to overlook
some of the potential *green lights*, and become your spouse's connoisseur, finding creative ways to meet their non-sexual needs— a
need to be shown affection, or a need to talk and be understood,
or a need to be supported, or a need to have quality time together.
Review the top ten-list from Chapter 11, knowing that the order of
importance is not set by you, but is determined by your spouse.

For Laura, she needed to step back and look at how she was meeting Tim's needs of feeling respected and supported, which were his
most important needs. Although his lack of sexual involvement was
not in response to Laura's lack of meeting his needs, she did begin
to build up resentments that colored her attitude toward Tim, resentments that leaked out in sarcastic and biting remarks. On the
RAM, you can see the interaction between the bonds of their relationship, and how the lowered levels of touch seemed to pull down
her trust, rearranging her trust-picture of Tim with more negative
images coming to the forefront of her mind (see figure 15.1).

Being responsible for your attitude toward your partner is easy
when your partner is doing everything you like! But Laura needed
to work on keeping a positive attitude of trust even though she had
unmet sexual needs. This is not to say that the imbalance that existed between her and Tim was justified, because the design for a
healthy relationship is not one partner giving while the other holds
back, but *mutual fulfillment*. But still, Laura needed to work harder
on her expressions of support and respect while she also lovingly
and firmly voiced the need in their marriage to address the issues in
their sexual relationship.

Step Three: Take ownership of the sexual needs of your spouse.

On the other hand, if your drive is lower than your spouse, then your greatest challenge may be to take a joint ownership of the sexual needs and wants in your relationship. You say, "What do you mean?"

A few years ago, I was training and certifying instructors to teach my marriage course, and when I came to this section, a middle-aged woman, Diane stood up and said, "It took me about ten years into my marriage before I learned this."

She explained that Marc, her husband, was a Pastor, and that he had a fairly high drive, but she did not—and so they had countless arguments about timing and frequency. But sometime around her early thirties, she felt that God impressed on her that she viewed the sexual relationship as her husband's responsibility, and that she was not taking any ownership of her own sexuality or what happened in their sex life.

So, one evening, she privately began to write about taking a part in the ownership of their sexual relationship. She wrote what she liked sexually, ways to please him and that he could please her, how she would like to be approached, and the ways that she could excite him.

When completed, she looked over her notes and said to herself, "Darn, this is good!"

So, she decided to give it to her husband. But she wanted to do it in a way that he would appreciate. She knew he left for church early every morning to have his alone time with God, and she also knew that he read his Bible during that time because it was always marked with a bookmark. So, after he had gone to bed for the night, she slipped this note in his Bible where he would discover it the next morning.

When Marc left for the office, you can be sure that Diane was wide awake, only pretending to sleep. She checked the clock. His drive to church was fifteen minutes, so she figured she would hear from him in about twenty.

But when twenty minutes came and went, and then thirty, and then forty, she began to feel dejected. She had worked hard on this, and now it didn't even seem to matter to him.

Just as she was about to call Marc and give him a stern talking-to, she heard the racing motor of a car in the distance. She sprung out of bed and peered out the window just in time to catch her husband squealing the tires to a halt as he jumped out of his car... half undressed. When he burst into their bedroom, he exclaimed, "This morning, I had the best time with God that I have ever had."

That was the beginning of Diane taking joint responsibility for their sexual relationship and her husband's sexual needs. She told our class that she would only give us a couple of the ways that she has continued to spice up their sex life even though she had such a low sex drive herself.

She began to hide little sticky notes for him, each one having a sexually inviting suggestion. She taped one to the inside of his car visor, stuck another in a pocket in his briefcase, and wrapped a third inside one of his socks. She continued over the years to hide these notes in every obscure place you can imagine. And whenever he found one, she was ready!

One night, when watching a movie together, he got up to get something to eat. A little later, he slipped away to do something in his office. But the third time he interrupted their movie time and headed into the dining room, she said, "What on earth are you doing??"

With his head under the dining room table she heard him mutter, "There's got to be a sticky note here somewhere."

She ended by saying something quite profound. She said, "You may think I did this just for my husband... but not really. It was that I had to come to a point where I took ownership of my sexuality and our sexual closeness. It really wasn't about fulfilling his agenda, it was much more about making it mine.

Step Four: Talk regularly about your sex life.

I want to end where I began. Do not slip into the trap of not talking about this area of your marriage, or of finding yourselves stuck in the "shut down" mode. Michele Wiener Davis wrote in The Sex-Starved Marriage:

> I have had many high drive spouses tell me that the problem in their marriage was not the differences in their sex drives as much as it was the fact that their partners were dismissive of their feelings and unwilling to do anything at all to address the issue.[1]

This is why your couple huddles are so vital and necessary. They will protect you from the dangerous silent stalemate of no longer discussing an area of your marriage that is out of balance and causing frustration and hurt. When you talk through the RAM in your huddles, you quickly cover all major areas of your relationship, both the sexual and the nonsexual.

Over the years, and through the different stages of your family, many things can change. And these changes will most likely impact your sex life. In each stage, couples tend to think that their relationship will improve just as soon as they enter the next stage. But what they find is that every stage of married life has its own unique challenges, including those with their sexual intimacy. During the child-raising years, there are hectic schedules, work-related stressors, and constant distractions that can pull you two apart. However, during the empty nest stage of marriage, there are other challenges to your sexual relationship that can be even more challenging: illnesses, medications, menopause, and sexual changes that lower libido and the ability to experience arousal and climax.

But when you face these challenges together, you can talk

through any of your changes, being committed to **mutually ful-filling** each other in creative and meaningful ways that will keep your sexual bond vibrant and strong. It is only when you stop having huddles, and give up on actively running your relationship, that there is a real danger from any of life's slow leaks. Making a commitment to never stop having huddles based on the RAM will secure that you will never give up on any area of your relationship, especially your sexual intimacy.

What I said in an earlier chapter is important to repeat. If you are unable to make a significant improvement in some problem area of your relationship after four-six months, then you should seek some help outside of yourselves— book, an online search, a physician, a counselor, a faith-professional—someone you trust who can provide insights and guidance that will move you toward an understanding and resolution of the difficulty you face.

You are responsible to actively run your relationship. Your relationship does not run itself, and it is not self-correcting. But now that you understand the major bonds of your relationship, and have a plan for regularly reviewing how you are growing and sustaining those areas, you can determine when you need to bring in a resource outside of yourselves to help. The key is to continue to be the ones who run your relationship, making the small (and big) adjustments to rebalance and strengthen the bonds that hold you close.

The next section of this book is designed to provide you with practical ideas, activities, and interactive exercises to use in your huddles, and to help you realign your relationship bonds during those inevitable, unbalancing experiences of life.

the huddle guide

guide

written by Morgan Cutlip, Ph.D.

Chapter 16: Practical Help for Your Huddles

Your huddles are the regular time you set to review your relationship, looking at what you are doing well, and what you need to either increase or to add to your relationship. Here are a few key points to maximizing the effectiveness of your huddles.

Expect to have some unmet personal needs in you, and in your spouse's life.

I want you to be relieved to know that your relationship, like ALL relationships, has ups and downs, fluctuating feelings of closeness, fulfillment, satisfaction, and intimacy... and that it is NORMAL to become imbalanced by life's good times, challenges and failures.

Relationship skills are necessary to maintain relationship bonds.

No one has mastered all relationship skills. So be receptive to working on a skill that will make you more effective in loving your spouse, and maintaining each of the five bonds of your relationship. Sometimes, your huddles will highlight a communication or relationship skill that one or both of you will want to search out, read more about, and work on so that your relationship continues to grow.

Do not stop having regular huddles.

Your marriage is a journey, and the RAM can be your relationship GPS. And it is in these regular huddles that you will frequently "reroute" your relationship in small ways to keep you on course of meeting each other's needs, and staying close.

Keep your huddles brief and positive.

Your huddles should be brief (20-30 minutes), positive, frequent (every week or two), and a time for review, and making plans for your relationship. Your huddle is a review of the last week or two, and planning meeting for the next upcoming weeks. If you have major topics or issues that need to be addressed, set a time and date when you can focus on them. Huddles are not a time to complain about things your spouse does or does not do. You can bring issues to the table for discussion, but your goal is to address things before they fester and develop into deep wounds that can hurt your relationship. Huddles are designed to keep you two on the same page. Make it your mission to go into your huddles with a spirit of humility, and with the goal of really hearing what your spouse has to say.

Use the RAM chart to help structure your huddles.

I want you to be empowered by understanding what EXACTLY IS your relationship, and that the RAM chart defines the major connections or bonds between you two, and gives you a common language to explain how you see your relationship, and what you would like to strengthen your relationship. Your huddles are formatted in five steps, one for each of the major bonds of your relationship as portrayed in the RAM. A good guideline is to take about five minutes for each step.

Begin your huddles with a prayer.

If you share a faith and feel comfortable with praying together, then begin and end your huddles with a brief pray. This will help to put you both in a spiritual mindset so that you relate with grace and love.

Here is a quick summary of each of the five steps of your huddles.

KNOW: Catch Up about what has happened with each other since your last huddle. Review what has been happening, and look for anything you need to talk about that you have overlooked or just lacked the time to discuss? If too much to talk about right in your huddle, set a time to address it.

TRUST: Patch Up your trust and positive attitudes by taking time in every huddle to look at your spouse, and tell them how they have blessed you with things that they have said and done since your last huddle. And if there were any misunderstanding or conflicts, affirm your apologies and commitment to resolve those issues.

RELY: Dream Up what you would like to do before your next huddle to meet some of the needs and wants of your spouse. You can use the top-10 list from this book, and also make your own top-10 list. Together, you can be the connoisseurs of each other. There will always be something that is lacking, but these deficits become the opportunities for you to give to your spouse, and to do enjoyable things together before your next huddle. Be sure to put your plans on your calendars!

COMMIT: Back Up each other by looking ahead on your calendars, and finding ways to support each other in your upcoming responsibilities and activities. If there are needed changes with how you are supporting each other and dividing up the responsibilities of your home, then make a date to talk more in-depth about this.

TOUCH: Build Up each other by taking some extra time to talk about your affection, romance and sexual intima-cy... what you appreciate, and what you would like to do before your next huddle. Express your love in words and in affection as you wrap up your time together.

Chapter 17: Step 1: Catch Up (Know)

The first step of your huddle is about your communication and how you have been staying in the know. Here are some topics and techniques for your first step.

1. Establish Regular Talk Times

Staying in the know requires that you and your spouse have regular times to talk in your routine. This does not mean a minute-long exchange of, "How was your day?" "Good" over screaming kids or a blaring TV. Set a designated talk time for 30-minutes or more. And make sure it is an uninterrupted time to just catch up with your partner. And try to have this talk time daily if possible.

Here are some questions to get you started talking about your talk times.

- Do we have regular talk times?
- How have they been going?
- What usually interrupts these times?
- What changes need to be made to make sure we keep this in our schedules?
- What are some additional ways to keep this a priority?
- What reminders will help us keep our talk time?
- What topics do each of us like to talk about in a talk time?

Here are some ideas for when you can have your talk time.
- After the kids go to bed.
- Early in the morning before work.
- During a drive in the car.
- Take a walk together.
- On a date night.
- On your lunch hour.
- At dinner.
- After dinner.

2. Talk about how you listen

Being a good listener is a major part of good communication. When your spouse is talking to you, there are generally four ways you can listen and respond. They can also be woven together in combinations when you listen. They are all good, but often your spouse would prefer one over another. Talk about each one and how you would like your spouse to let you know which response they would prefer.

> **Empathetic listening.** You listen by supporting and sympathizing with your spouse.
>
> **Appreciative.** You listen to express appreciation for your partner, what they have said or done, and what they are experiencing.
>
> **Reflective.** You listen inquisitively; you ask questions or prompt for more details.
>
> **Suggestive.** You listen to help, fix, offer advice or problem-solve.

A real common listening style for men (and many women) is to want to *fix* whatever is going on with your spouse. However, this can be viewed as unsympathetic or condescending. Be sure to practice more of the 1-3 styles of listening. And when you do offer suggestions, ask first to see if that is something your spouse would like.

How to ask for a listening style:

"I would really like some ideas to solve_____ issue."

"Please don't try to fix this, I would just like to vent about

_____ ."

How to ask what listening style is preferred:

"Are you telling me about this and wanting me to just listen and know what has been happening with you, or do you want help or ideas from me."

"I had an idea about what you could do, but I am not sure if you want my ideas or just want me to listen and understand what's happening with you."

3. Talk about how you talk

Here are some questions to talk about the ways you both talk with each other.

- How has the quality of our communication been?
- Is there anything you would like me to ask more about?
- Is there anything you've had on your mind that you've wanted to talk about?
- When we see each other after a day at work, how would you like our conversation to go? Do you want some quiet time, or do you like to jump right into talking to one another?
- How can I better help you to feel like I'm tracking what's going on in your world when we get really busy?

For those of you who struggle at times to come up with things to talk to your partner about, try these conversation starters.

- Tell me about something good that happened today?
- What was your favorite part of the day?
- Was there anything on your mind today?
- Tell me about something that occupied your thoughts today.
- Is there anything that you wanted to get done today, but didn't?
- How's your (friend, mom, dad, boss, co-worker, etc.)? Give me an update on them.
- What's been the best thing that has happened this week? Tell me about it.
- Did anything frustrate you today? What happened?
- If you could have anything taken off your plate, what would it be?
- Tell me about something that happened today that was funny.
- Is there anything that I can do to help you tonight?

Chapter 18: Step 2: Patch Up (Trust)

This step in your huddle is all about patching up any negative attitudes you have held toward your spouse. This does not mean that you immediately scan for negatives. In fact, the starting point is to focus on the positives!

1. Count your blessings

This is something you should do in every huddle. Look at your spouse and think through the time since your last huddle (or the last week or two). Describe what your spouse has said or done that you really appreciate. Try to be descriptive. Also, think about your spouse's strengths that prompt them to talk or act in this positive way. Tie their actions in with those strengths. Let them know how they have blessed you in those ways. You may want to share just one positive, and then have your spouse share a positive about you. And then take your second turn, and think of another positive. Try to outdo each other in counting the ways your spouse has blessed you!

2. Get back on track

There will be times when even the best of intentions will not protect you from the unexpected turn a discussion can take. Here are a couple of ideas if you find yourself in one of those conversations.

"I was just trying to be helpful."

While you may have thought that you provided your partner with a helpful response or told them what they needed to hear, apparently it wasn't what they wanted to hear. So, take a moment and check in with your partner, and ask what type of response they would find most helpful. Explain that you meant well, but understand that sometimes your spouse just wants... support.... advice.... empathy.... encouragement.

"Do you really want to bring that up right now?"

You are enjoying your talk time and then you find yourself in a sensitive conversation. Before you know it, things feel tense and your wonderful talk time is now becoming an argument. This is not the intention of a huddle, so do what you can to table that discussion. Quickly wrap up this conversation and set a time to talk about it in the future. If your issue is one that does not need to be discussed anymore, work towards patching up this issue by affirming your apology, forgiveness, and your positive trust-picture of your spouse.

3. Apologize with meaning

As you work through your huddle, know that there may be times that you will have to say, "I'm sorry," or times that you may have to "let go" of things from the past that are still creeping into your thinking and causing a bad attitude. The following skill of apology will help you to navigate this section of the huddle.

Apologizing is a necessary skill in marriage. It is more than just saying the words, "I'm sorry." And it often needs to be repeated, just to affirm your remorse and understanding of what you had said or done.

STEP 1: Acknowledge what your partner is saying you did or said that bothered him or her.

STEP 2: Apologize for what you did or said or for how you came across. "I am sorry for ———————— " Or, "I am sorry for coming across as _____ when I did or said _____ ."

STEP 3: Briefly explain your motives and your perspective. Sometimes you can stop after step two, but if you feel really compelled to explain, then make it brief! Watch out for using "but" after you apologize—it will negate your apology. So, explain if you must, but make sure your focus is on the apology first, and then on clarifying your motive.

STEP 4: If you explained your motive, apologize again! Especially after you said, "but." For example, "I am sorry when I said _____ . What I really meant was _____ , but I am sorry that I came across in an unappreciative way, and hurt your feelings."

If you are the one being apologized to, work to accept the apology. If your partner has humbled himself or herself and said that they are sorry, do not brush that off. Do not minimize it, or dismiss it. Accept it. Apologizing is hard. So, receive it, believe it and then accept it.

4. Become your spouse's defense attorney

This technique is a must for when you and your spouse are in a conflict, and you can even practice it in just your day-to-day life.

In conversations, it is common for you to look for an opportunity to respond: jump in, tell your side of the story, give your opinion, or just change the conversation completely.

Instead, try to listen as if you are the defense attorney of your spouse. Listen to what they are telling you and then, state their case back to them as if you were their representative. When you state their case, work to convey both the facts of what they were telling you as well as the emotion behind what was going on for them. If you label or describe the emotion incorrectly, do not make a big deal of it. Your spouse will most likely correct that for you, so don't get defensive. Their correction will help you to gain a deeper understanding of their experience.

This works wonders during a conflict, and can diffuse the tension so that your partner feels like you are really getting what they are saying. This technique can be used even when you do not agree with their position or perspective. When you explain your spouse's points back to him or her, it shows your spouse that you were really listening and working to understand his or her perspective.

In non-conflictual times, during day-to-day conversations, this technique will help you to slow down, and focus on what your spouse is saying. You will be able to go beyond the typical "uhh huhhs" and "gotchas" to better understand your spouse, and to make them feel understood.

5. "Refresh" That Attitude

This is one of the most important skills in marriage, although it is something you do more in your own mind than with your spouse. You may believe that you are responsible for your own attitude toward your spouse, but too many times we operate by the "blame game," rather than by self-responsibility. Although your attitude toward your partner will autocorrect at times, most times you will have to put some concerted effort towards improving how you think about your spouse. For the times that you need an attitude adjustment, use these four steps below.

1. TAKE RESPONSIBILITY FOR YOUR OWN ATTITUDE

It is so common to blame others for "making" us feel certain ways, but ultimately, you are in charge of your attitude. The first step will always be to own your attitude toward your spouse.

2. REMEMBER YOUR PARTNER'S STRENGTHS

There are times when your partner's strengths become overshadowed by your negativity. It is at those times that you must call to mind their strengths.

3. REFLECT ON YOUR PARTNER'S STRENGTHS

Remembering your partner's strengths is not enough, you must reflect on how those strengths positively benefit and enrich your life.

4. EXPRESS IN WORDS and ACTIONS YOUR APPRECIATION OF THE WAYS YOUR PARTNER BLESSES YOU

The last step is to tell your partner that you appreciate him or her, and the ways that they bless you. This step is critical because it is important for you to get out of your own head and start acting on a more positive attitude. And when you express your appreciation, it isn't enough to just say, "I appreciate you." Be specific about what qualities you appreciate, and how they have benefitted you.

Chapter 19: Step 3: Dream Up (Rely)

This step in your huddle is all about how you and your spouse meet each other's needs, work together to fulfill the responsibilities of your home and relationship, and plan out your togetherness. Be sure to have fun as you dream up things that you would like to do together.

There are a few guidelines that are important to follow during your huddles, and will help you to maintain a healthy reliance on each other.

Don't get defensive.

I have explained that it is normal for needs to go unmet. Just because you're working hard to meet the needs of your spouse, does not mean that all their needs are being met at all points in time. Life is busy. You may be doing great at helping around the house or taking things off your spouse's plate, but at the same time, you could be lacking in romantic gestures or expressions of appreciation. That's OK. If this went on too long, then a slow leak could lead to big blowout. But if you have the understanding that not everything can be taken care of every day or every week, and that as you feed one area of your relationship, some other area is getting hungry. So, go into your huddle expecting your spouse to need something from you rather than being offended that they are not happy with all that you have been doing for them.

What you need today may not be what you need tomorrow.

Needs change. This can happen because you have a change in your schedule, life circumstances, responsibility load, illness, age, and the list goes on. Maybe you have become a master at meeting certain needs of your spouse only to have them say that they need something different. Try to remember that this is normal, that needs change, and that it is not an insult or criticism of how good of a job you are doing when they want something more, or something different.

Express your needs and wants with grace.

My mother used to say, "It is not what you said, it is how you said it." Very often, the issues described in the first two guidelines can be prompted by how you bring up an unmet need, a new desire, or a wish for more of what your spouse has already been doing. Couch your requests within an appreciation of what your spouse has already been doing for you. Let them know that you "give them credit" for all the ways they show their love and care for you. You can even remind them that there will always be something, and to not take this need as a failure, or a shortcoming on their part. Remember, a graceful word and a loving touch can often soothe a defensive spouse.

Put your wishes in order.

The fourth guideline is that some needs are more important than others to your spouse. We all have needs. Most of us have a need for love, support, help, and empathy. But there are some needs that matter more at one time versus another. Talk about what needs mean the most to you. Ask your spouse what is most important to him or her. Here are some ideas on determining which needs and wants are the priorities.

- Ask!
- Pay attention to how your spouse meets your needs. This is most likely what he or she would like most from you.
- Think about your spouse's previous complaints, this may clue you in.
- Think back to things you've done for your partner, what really seemed to do it for them?

I just want a little more of the good you are giving.

The final guideline is that sometimes your spouse may need "more" of something. This concept can so easily lead to conflict if it isn't understood. For example,

> Wife: *"Babe, I wish you would let me know that you appreciate me a little more."*

> Husband: *"Seriously, I am always telling you "thank you." And I've been trying to do this more and more, but you're never satisfied. Maybe you're just a little too needy for compliments."*

So, the wife is asking for more of something her husband is already doing. And because it is one of her most desired needs, to be affirmed and appreciated, she would like him to do it more often. But her husband interpreted this as, "I'm not doing a good job meeting her need." He then, became defensive and turned it around to be her issue.

This is a very common pattern among couples and could be avoided if spouses had the mindset that it is normal to ask for more of a good thing, and that asking for more does not mean that one spouse is failing, or is not doing anything at all.

Get busy with your top-ten list.

Take each of the ten categories in this book from chapter 11, and dream up things you would like to do. Reminisce about times that you have enjoyed something you did together in a category in the top-10 list. Make a commitment to meet your spouse's most meaningful needs over the next few weeks. If you struggle knowing how to do this, go online and search out some sites. Once you have picked some ways to let your spouse know you care, set reminders in your phone to put them into action.

Chapter 20: Step 4: Back Up (Commit)

Commitment is a force in your relationship that bonds you together even when you are physically apart. It prompts sacrifice, and a desire to make your spouse a higher priority. And commitment helps you to persevere, even when life is hard. Commitment is also how we show our spouse that we have his or her back. This step of your huddle is to express your commitment in practical ways.

1. Daily expressions of your commitment

Here are some questions to talk about that helps you know how to put commitment into action from your huddles.

- What is one way this week that you felt I was there for you? If you didn't feel it, what was an opportunity that I missed?
- How do you like to receive support from me (i.e. words, pep talks, actions, initiative, etc.)?
- How can I better show my support for you?

Here are some ideas of things you can do to express your commitment.

- Throughout this week, think of one thing you can sacrifice in your own life and replace it with something you can do to take care of your spouse, or make their life easier.
- Come up with new ways to let your spouse know that you are thinking of him or her throughout the day when you are gone. For example, a midday text letting your spouse know that they are on your mind. Leave a note in a place where they will find it later.

2. Celebrate your victories

Take some time in you huddle to talk about any challenging situation you successfully went through. This can be something small or relatively significant. Avoid the overwhelming topics that stir up too much emotion. Identify the specific ways your spouse supported you that you greatly appreciated—what they did, what they said, how they handled situations. This will help you to express your appreciation, affirm your commitment, and learn how your spouse likes your support during times of stress.

3. Trust and Forgiveness

Whenever you experience some breakdown of trust, no matter how small, it is necessary to practice two relationship skills that help to heal and strengthen your relationship. These are forgiveness, and the rebuilding of trust. Although both have some overlap, there are distinct differences, and both are essential for a full reconciliation.

Here are some topics to talk through with forgiveness.

- What you would like from each other when you have your feelings hurt.
- How would you like your spouse to talk with you about something that hurt you?
- How would you like your spouse to ask for your forgiveness?

- What is forgiveness, and how do you do it?

Here are some topics to talk through with rebuilding trust.
- What are areas of trust that you and your spouse should talk about and strengthen?
- What can each of you do for the other to help that spouse feel more trusting and secure?
- What would help each of you to feel more important and a higher priority to your spouse.

If you are facing a more serious breach of trust, affirm your commitment to move through the journey of forgiving and rebuilding trust, and persevere until you reach a destination of reconciliation and healing.

Chapter 21: Step 5: Build Up (Touch)

In this step of your huddle, you and your spouse will focus on conversations about your sex-life, your displays of affection, your romance and your overall physical relationship.

Something to keep in mind throughout these conversations is that for some people, sex begins long before you arrive in the bedroom. Sexual intimacy is intertwined with feelings of closeness, fulfillment, support and overall satisfaction in the relationship. During the third step of your huddle, you may have talked about your sexual relationship in the context of romance and other non-sexual needs and wants. However, the fifth step of your huddle specifically focuses on your sexual closeness, particularly because this is such a vital area of your marriage relationship.

Here are some conversations to have in your huddle:

1. Talk about your sex drives.

There is a large range from high to low of the sex drive. Talk about where each of you fall on the spectrum—you may want to rate your drive by a number scale (like 1-10), or by the frequency that you would prefer to have sexual activity in your relationship.

2. There are many things that can impact on your drive.

If your drive has fluctuated or changed, what are some of the contributing factors?

3. Describe any differences between you and your spouse in your sex drives.

How would you like to become involved in the sexual act when you're not in the mood? It is important to note that often, the spouse with the lower drive will engage in sex when not in the mood, but their partner with a higher drive is initiating. So, talk about this. And if you have the lower drive, how can your spouse help you get in the mood when you're not. What can you do to participate when you are not really feeling it?

4. Talk about how your sexual relationship fits in with the other bonds in your relationship.

Is it in balance with your communication and the ways you keep up with knowing each other? Is it in balance with your attitudes of respect and admiration? Are you interacting in positive ways to meet the nonsexual needs of each other? Many times, difficulties with a sexual relationship are prompted by struggles in other areas of your marriage relationship. On the other hand, there are some-times that struggles in your sexual relationship will be the source of problems in other areas of your marriage.

5. How would you like to approach and be approached sexually?

Let your spouse know how you like to be approached when he or she is in the mood. Talk about how you will let your spouse know when you are in the mood. Discuss who usually initiates, and how can the person who initiates less work toward initiating more?

6. Decide on acceptable ways to say, "not now."

It is a fact that there will be times where one of you is just not in the mood. Talk about how you can say, "no" without upsetting your spouse, or causing them to feel rejected.

7. Discuss what sexual activities you would like in your relationship.

Talk about how adventurous you would like to be. What are sexual preferences do you have, and what would you like to do or try?

8. Share with your spouse ways that they get you in the mood.

What are some things that your spouse does for you that really make you feel desired? How do you flirt, and how would you like your spouse to flirt with you?

9. Discuss your expectations of boundaries.

Talk about what boundaries you considerable acceptable with others. What do you consider acceptable and unacceptable in opposite sex and same sex relationships? How boundaries would you like your partner to practice in social settings? With co-workers or job situations? With your friends?

10. Explore your values and beliefs about sex and affection.

Discus what you've learned about sex and affection from your upbringing. Talk about your family's attitudes about sex.

11. Talk about family planning.

Discuss your values and expectations around family planning, and your desire for children.

the con-clusion

Chapter 22: The Conclusion

It is our hope that you now feel empowered to actively run your marriage relationship, and that the RAM has provided you with a job description of what it means to keep your relationship growing, balanced and fulfilling. Your relationship is dynamic, and will be continually impacted by the events of your life. But you do not have to feel like your relationship is a victim of life circumstances, because now that you know what are the major bonds of your relationship, and you have an interactive tool that you can use to evaluate where you are strong and where you are lacking, you have gained the ability to make the small adjustments that can help you to avoid the big pitfalls.

There is an old commercial that has a tagline, "Life comes at you fast." And when you are not having regular times of talking openly about your relationship, and making those necessary recalibrations, then your vulnerability to growing apart slowly increases, overlooking a build-up of frustrations and irritations, and running the risk of crashing into a major crisis. Most marital crises do not occur in a vacuum, but rather are preceded by a long period of neglected areas in one or more of the dynamic bonds described in the RAM.

This is why we firmly believe that there is just one key to a successful relationship... and that is to have regular huddles based on the RAM. If you stay faithful with genuinely reviewing your relationship in the five areas of the RAM, and working together to identify and improve what is lacking or needed, then your relationship will continue to quickly rebalance, and over time, will stay vibrant and strong. And if you become stuck in some area of your relationship, you will either fix it, or find resources outside of you two to help make it better. Maintaining regular huddles will protect you from neglecting or just tolerating a problem that could fester to eventually cripple your relationship.

So, keep your huddles. Set your goals. Make it happen. And know that as you put out this small amount of effort, you will gain a lifetime of happiness together.

From our hearts,

John Van Epp, Ph.D. and Morgan Cutlip, Ph.D.

the refer-
ences

Chapter 6

1 Keller, Timothy J. The Meaning of Marriage: Facing the Complexities of Commitment with the Wisdom of God. New York: Penguin Books, 2011.

Chapter 8

1 Zitzman, S.T. & Butler, M. H. (2009). Wives' experience of pornography use and concomitant deception as an attachment threat in the adult-pair relationship. Sexual Addiction and Compulsivity, 16, 210-240.

Chapter 10

1 Huston, T., Surra, C., Fitzgerald, N., & Cate, R. (1981). From courtship to marriage: Mate selection as an interpersonal process. In S. Duck & R. Gilmour (Eds.), Personal relationships, 2: Developing personal relationships (pp. 53–90). London: Academic Press.

2 Utne, M., Hatfield, E., Traupmann, J., & Greenbeger, D. (1984). Equity, marital satisfaction, and stability. Journal of Social and Personal Relationships, 1, 323–332.

3 excerpt from Van Epp, J. How to avoid falling in love with a jerk. McGraw-Hill. 2007.

Chapter 11

1 Gergen, Kenneth (Editor). Social Exchange: Advances in Theory and Practice. Springer, 2011.

2 excerpt from Van Epp, J. How to avoid falling in love with a jerk. McGraw-Hill. 2007.

Chapter 12

1 Waite, L., Browning, D., Doherty, W., Gallagher, M., Luo, Y., Stanley,

S. Does Divorce Make People Happy (2002). Institute for American Values.

2 Waite, L., Browning, D., Doherty, W., Gallagher, M., Luo, Y., Stanley, S. Does Divorce Make People Happy (2002). Institute for American Values, p. 5.

3 Hawkins, A. What Are They Thinking? A National Survey of Married Individuals Who Are Thinking About Divorce. A Report From The National Divorce Decision-Making Project. (2015). Provo, UT: Family Studies Center, Brigham Young University.

4 Keller, Timothy J. The Meaning of Marriage: Facing the Complexities of Commitment with the Wisdom of God. New York: Penguin Books, 2011.

Chapter 13

1 Fehr, B. (1988). Prototype Analysis of the Concepts of Love and Commitment. Journal of Personality and Social Psychology, 55, 557-579.

Chapter 14

1 Seven Reasons to be Skin-to-Skin with your Baby after Birth. https://www.mommypotamus.com/benefits-of-skin-to-skin

2 Floyd, K. (2014). Relational and Health Correlates of Affection Deprivation. Western Journal of Communication, 78, No. 4, July-September 2014, pp. 382-403.

3 Gulledge, A.K, Gulledge, M.H. & Stahmann, R.F. (2003). Romantic Physical Affection Types and Relationship Satisfaction. The American Journal of Family Therapy, 31, 233-242.

4 Winslow J.T., Hastings N., Carter C.S., Harbaugh C.R. & Insel T.R.

References

(1993). A role for central vasopressin in pair bonding in monogamous prairie voles, Nature, 365 (6446) 545-548. Young L.J. & Wang Z. (2004). The neurobiology of pair bonding, Nature Neuroscience, 7 (10) 1048-1054.

5 Bick, J., Grasso, D., Dozier, M., Bernard, K., and Simons, R. (2013). Foster Mother–Infant Bonding: Associations Between Foster Mothers' Oxytocin Production, Electrophysiological Brain Activity, Feelings of Commitment, and Caregiving Quality. Child Development, Vol 84, Number 3, p. 826-840.

Chapter 15

1 Wiener-Davis, Michele. The Sex-Starved Marriage. New York: Simon & Schuster, 2003.